How to be an
Everyday
Kitchen
Magician

Fabulous food for
almost free

How to be an Everyday Kitchen Magician

Fabulous food for almost free

RICHARD FOX

green books

First published in 2012 by

Green Books
Dartington Space, Dartington Hall,
Totnes, Devon TQ9 6EN

All photographs are by the author, except:
page 7: T. Cumberland
pages 9, 28, 38, 50, 76, 113, 136, 153: Jessica Holden
pages 19, 33, 59, 127, 149: JP Hedge Photography
pages 101, 107, 119: Jayne Jones

Design by Jayne Jones
Cover illustrations by Ellie Mains
Back cover photographs (top) by Jessica Holden

ISBN 978 0 85784 027 1

Printed on UPM Fine paper
by Latimer Trend, Plymouth, UK

Contents

The recipes

Author's note

For months, while I was compiling and writing this book, tucking into spontaneous lunches was delayed as I documented their creation and photographed the tantalising finished dishes before I could eat. Many of the recipes found in these pages represent actual forays into my fridge, freezer, cupboards and veg rack – not just to illustrate the principles in the book, but to feed me as I laboured over keyboard and camera.

But you, the public, have had an enormous influence on the shaping of this book. Over the last couple of years I have given hundreds of cooking demonstrations, and after every one I invite questions and ask people to come and talk to me, one-to-one, with their queries, thoughts and culinary dilemmas. As such, I have built up a pretty comprehensive picture of the most common conundrums: what and how to re-use and re-heat; how to par-cook and cook-and-chill; what ingredients can and can't be put to use – and have been able to enlighten and inform accordingly. All along my aim has been to help free you of the constraints of formal recipe cooking and to arm you with the techniques to create your own flavoursome concoctions with whatever you have available, without a second thought.

I hope this book will be a manual for inspiration and creativity – giving you the tools to be an everyday kitchen magician. The recipes should be seen simply as guidelines or reference points for creating your own bespoke dishes from your fridge contents, cupboard inhabitants and random leftovers. As such, there are numerous suggestions throughout for how a basic recipe concept can be added to, enhanced, adapted and personalised to create any number of tasty meals.

You, the public, have had an enormous influence on the shaping of this book.

The author supporting The Nottinghamshire Waste Partnership campaign.

Introduction

This book is so much more than a recipe book. In fact, it's about learning to cook without using recipes at all. It's all about making the most of what you have, reducing your waste dramatically, and learning how to create spontaneous, delicious dishes in minutes. It represents a food philosophy that will change your approach to cooking for ever, leaving you a better cook with more cash in your pocket. It's a journal of exploration, eureka discoveries and amazing taste sensations – all generated through a series of shifts in my own thinking over years of tireless cooking demonstrations.

These pages are filled with ingredients and leftovers that many of us would throw away without so much as a second thought, purely because of an expired 'best before' date or because that veg is looking just a little past it. Wrinkled peppers, greying carrots, bendy courgettes and blotchy celery are all part of the family of old-timers and has-beens that lives in the average household vegetable rack. (And let's not even go near the fridge salad drawer, lest we have a similar experience to Sigourney Weaver opening her refrigerator in *Ghostbusters*.) The truth is, however, that many of these tired-looking ingredients are not only perfectly usable but may actually be tastier than when in their pristine, 'supermarket-shelf' condition. And what about those irresistible 'buy one get one free' offers, which more often than not results in punnet-loads of perfectly good fruit being consigned to the bin?

Right: The perfect lunch – in under 5 minutes.

Moreover – while we're on the subject of supermarket-aisle opportunities – there's a host of thrifty and delicious dishes to be created from special-offer meat or fish, reduced in price as it approaches or hits its 'use by' date. If you can't cook it at once, you can always stick it straight in the freezer.

Finally, how many times do we scrape leftover cooked food into the bin just because we can't possibly imagine what to do with a couple of florets of broccoli, two spoonfuls of spag bol or a quarter-tin of tuna? What can and can't be re-heated? How do we cool down safely (the food, that is), in order to re-heat at a later date? In light of this, I've dedicated a whole chapter to cooked leftovers. The point is, why go out and buy yet more food when the chances are you've already got everything to hand to magic up something scrumptious?

Supporting roles in this book go to the dried herbs and spices hidden away in what I've christened 'the scary cupboard' – which is, more often than not, also home to various flours and pulses, the like of which you probably can't even name, let alone cook. So, it's time for a little demystification too. Face your fears, friends, and you'll find they go away. And of course there are the tins, packets and jars (usually in the cupboard next to the scary one) that get overlooked or neglected on the basis of seeming just too bland, boring or complicated. We're going to change that little misconception too.

These pages are filled with ingredients and leftovers that many of us would throw away without so much as a second thought.

This book will show you how to turn the dull, the rejected and the disaffected into spectacularly tasty and attractive dishes of the sort that you'd drool over in the finest gastro pub or restaurant, let alone relish as a spontaneous snack. It's not rocket science – in fact it's all a lot easier and less stressful than navigating the supermarket aisles on a Saturday afternoon. It's been a fantastic journey for me, and one that has not only made me a better cook and financial manager but also more environmentally aware.

A few more words about ingredients in this book: when I refer to eggs, I am always talking about free-range. Wherever possible, I'd encourage you to use sustainable fish and free-range meat. I don't advocate buying bargain-basement meat, but quality meat or fish is often bargain-priced as it approaches the date by which the supermarket has to ditch it. When I talk about seasoning, I'm always referring to salt and pepper – and preferably sea salt such as Maldon, and freshly ground black pepper. For frying, I use cold-pressed rapeseed oil. Failing that, you can now buy ordinary rapeseed oil, which will still do a top job and is substantially cheaper. Olive oil, when heated to a high temperature, creates trans fats – not good. Keep ordinary olive oil for low-temperature sautéing and the extra virgin for salad dressings, or for a dash over couscous, pasta or potato salad, or for making crostini and bread tart cases.

Aside from the fact that the ordinary so easily transforms into the extraordinary through everyday cooking processes, I would always encourage buying the best local and seasonal ingredients you can. Not only does this mean a huge reduction in those pesky food miles, but also that you're much more connected to where your food comes from and therefore have a greater sense of its value and are less likely to waste it. So, even though you may pay a little more for local produce, this fact alone will more than balance out the pennies.

Some remarkable and shocking facts*

We throw away **4.4 million tonnes** of good food and drink each year in the UK, all of which could have been eaten or drunk.

All this avoidable food and drink waste is responsible for the equivalent of **17 million tonnes of carbon dioxide** – that's like taking 1 in 5 cars off the road.

4.4 million tonnes of food and drink waste costs **£12 billion** – which equates to £480 per year for the average household, rising to around £680 per year for families with children.

* From 'New estimates for household food and drink waste in the UK, November 2011', WRAP (Waste and Resources Action Programme). Note: All these facts and figures relate to domestic household waste, not to any commercial waste such as that from supermarkets or the catering industry.

How to use this book

I have tried to organise this book in a user-friendly way, taking into account foods that are commonly wasted or that tend to hang around underused in our cupboards and fridges. So, recipes are listed under the most perishable ingredient or the food you are most likely to want to use up. For example, Spanish tortilla uses eggs, onions and potatoes. But it is listed under 'potatoes' because it's those sprouty potatoes in your veg rack that you are likely to be gazing at blankly, hoping for some noble inspiration.

One of the main aims of the book is to free you from regimented recipes, so practically all of the recipes are intended to be interpreted and adapted as you please. Throughout, I have suggested alternative ingredients and configurations. For example, whatever-you-want flan can be filled with cheese, veg, meat or fish; smoked haddock cauliflower cheese is equally delicious with bacon or sausage. Even standard sauces, such as white sauce, can be adapted in imaginative ways to create umpteen concoctions. To help navigate you through this exciting maze of flavour possibilities, each chapter also includes references to recipes in other chapters that use, or could use, the same ingredients.

The bottom line is, read the recipes with an open mind and a hungry heart, and they *will* reward you.

Change your thinking

It's all very well banging on about the virtues of not wasting food, using up old veg and keeping vigil over the hidden corners of the fridge like an over-zealous traffic warden. I've been immersed in this world for years and I still have to give myself a little nudge now and then when I can't be bothered to wrap the last remnants of fresh herbs in dampened kitchen paper for extra life.

The change jar principle

Changes in behaviour and habits, however simple, never come naturally or easily. The secret is to start changing the way you think – a kind of journey of the mind as much as the kitchen. As all the self-help, wealth-generating books in the world will tell you, every theory and achievement starts with a single thought in somebody's mind. So here's one I want to share with you: would you go around consigning all your saved bits of change to the bin? I very much doubt it. I keep a change jar in my hallway, and when it's full I haul it down to the supermarket and empty it into one of those giant change-eating machines that exchange it for a little slip of paper, which you then convert to pounds. It's like getting free money – and how good does that feel? Well, start thinking of those little morsels of leftover food and everyday ingredients stashed in the fridge, freezer, cupboards and veg rack as those little bits of change.

To bin or not to bin?

In this book I will show you how seemingly past-it veg still have a huge amount to offer: what used to be binned will be seen in a completely different light. And the effort that goes into implementing a few techniques to make food last longer is certainly no more effort than visiting the giant change monster. In fact, as you get into the swing of things you'll find that tedious and pricey shopping hours become

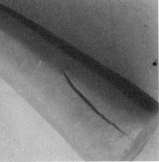

It may look past it, but scratch beneath the surface . . .

sharply reduced. Statistically, you'll save in the region of £600 a year. Now that's what I call food for thought.

The *Ready Steady Cook* principle

So, having saved those little morsels from premature binning, how do you take the leap to creating quick, easy and delicious meals from them? Again, this involves a simple shift in thinking – a more lateral approach to cooking than the traditional recipe formula. The next time you're searching for a little culinary inspiration from seemingly nothing, imagine you are a contestant in *Ready Steady Cook*. Good dishes generally don't involve a complex array of weird and wonderful ingredients. Quite the contrary in fact. Think about some of those famous recipes that have stood the test of time: hollandaise sauce, mayonnaise, Caesar salad, salad Niçoise, risotto. These are big-hitting, top-end restaurant stalwarts that have achieved gastronomic immortality – the Monroes of the food world that make the latest *Big Brother* celebrity look like a flash-in-the-pan fad diet. The most 'exotic' ingredient in that list of recipes is walnuts.

★ *Good dishes generally don't involve a complex array of weird and wonderful ingredients. In fact, quite the contrary is true.*

Salsatastic!

From this . . .   *. . . to this in minutes*

It's amazing how far stuff goes when you start chopping, dicing and grating, while just a little imagination can create the most gourmet combos from seemingly boring basics. This fantastic collection of simple appetisers doesn't even require any cooking, and adding lime juice before refrigeration slows down the deterioration that would be taking place if the fresh ingredients were left sitting in your veg rack and fruit bowl. Simply combine the ingredients, cover and then chill in the fridge. Check out the crostini recipe on page 54 for the perfect accompaniment.

Mango and courgette

half a mango (skinned, stoned and chopped)
1 small courgette, finely diced
juice of half a lime
1 tsp finely chopped fresh coriander
¼ tsp chilli flakes, crushed then finely chopped
pinch of salt and pepper

Apple and celery

1 apple, finely diced
1 celery stick, finely diced
juice of half a lime
2 tsp finely chopped fresh coriander
pinch of salt and pepper

Carrot and kidney bean

quarter or half a carrot, finely grated
220g tin kidney beans, rinsed, drained
and finely chopped or pulsed in a food
processor
half a red onion, finely diced
1 tsp finely chopped fresh coriander
1 tsp olive oil
pinch of chilli flakes
pinch of salt and pepper

Tomato and red onion

3 ripe tomatoes, deseeded and finely
chopped
half a red onion, finely diced
2 tsp fresh coriander, finely chopped
juice of half a lime
pinch of salt and pepper

Good cooking originates in the home

Classic recipes such as Caesar salad and salad Niçoise may have wound their way
into top-end restaurants based on their taste credentials, but the foundation of
great cooking and eating is not to be found in the hallowed dining rooms of the
world's greatest chefs. It's to be found in the homes of ordinary people – who, due
to economic circumstances, are forced to make the very best of what they have.
We live in a world where necessity is the mother of invention: the finest suppers
emerge from simple, ordinary ingredients – and, more often than not, from the
cheapest cuts, the offcuts and by-products of premium parts. Sushi evolved from
utilising vinegar-infused rice as a preserving layer between pieces of fish before
refrigeration was introduced. Fish and chips – Britain's most popular dish – came
about because deep-frying in batter was a means to disguise off-flavour fish prior
to refrigeration and freezing.

The beauty of this book is that it offers a whole stack of recipes you'll be able to
cook straight away with what you already have. And don't think that this in any way
diminishes the flavour or gastronomic quality of the finished dish. If I thought that
any of these recipes fell into the category of boring, uninspiring fodder purely to
take the edge off your hunger, they would have been consigned to the bin. Basic
everyday food does not have to mean boring. Let's celebrate creativity born of
frugality and environmental awareness – a return to discovery of flavour.

Basic essentials

This isn't about rushing out to buy the latest NASA-technology pans or super-sharp knives that could cut through rock. Having said that, it is worth investing in good-quality pans and knives – and cost is the best guide here – as they will contribute to your enjoyment of cooking and last a lifetime. I like to use RUN Cookware pans, which are made out of heavy-gauge, hand-cast aluminium. They heat quickly and evenly, making them more energy-efficient than other kinds of metallic cookware, and they are also highly durable. In addition to decent pans and knives, the checklist below contains most of the essential cooking accessories that you are likely to need for the recipes in this book.

Checklist

- **Griddle pan:** This ridged grill pan will convert tired old veg into appetising discs and ribbons of goodness in seconds.
- **Grater:** A swift shredding can transform the smallest morsel into a mountain.
- **Jug blender:** A must for soups and smoothies. Cleaning is a doddle – always a key factor in what gets consigned to the graveyard of kitchen appliances and what stays in regular use on the worktop.
- **Lemon zester:** Become a zestaholic. Utilise that intensely fragrant citrusy skin to add a kick and extra flavour dimension to all manner of meat, fish and salad dishes.
- **Muffin tin:** The ultimate edible vessel creator. From mini Yorkshire puddings to bread tart cases, you'll never be short of free finger food.
- **Permanent marker pen:** I always keep a marker pen next to the freezer so I can quickly label foods with the contents and date before freezing. The most obvious stuff in its unfrozen state becomes a blur of unrecognisability in its frozen form. The date will allow you to operate stock rotation if you end up

You don't need very sophisticated tools to create culinary masterpieces.

with more than one of the same. Six months is about the maximum shelf life for anything.

- **Airtight plastic containers with lids:** Keep single- or double-portion-sized square or rectangular containers (they fit in the fridge and freezer more efficiently). A few little ones are always useful for chopped, fresh herbs, roast garlic and random bits of prepared vegetables.
- **Stick blender with bowl and whisk attachment:** Worth its weight in exotic spices! This piece of kit will become indispensable in a matter of months, converting stale bread into perfect breadcrumbs, old tins of beans into delicious dips, and so much more.
- **Mug:** A standard-sized mug is useful for quick and easy measuring.
- **Tablespoon:** A universal standard measure to save faffing around with scales. Equivalent to four teaspoons.
- **Dessertspoon:** Another handy measure. Equivalent to two teaspoons.

Other useful bits

- **Speed peeler** (a 'Y'-shaped peeler with a mini built-in scoop for digging out those pesky potato eyes)
- **Fine sieve and colander**
- **Ladle**
- **Potato ricer** (like a giant garlic press for perfect mash)
- **Baking parchment**
- **Cling film**
- **Tin foil**
- **Food processor** (like the stick blender with bowl attachment, but bigger)

Principles for 'non-recipe', waste-free cooking

As I keep saying (reinforcement is a marvellous learning tool!), the main aim here is to be able to create instant dishes from whatever you have to hand. It's the ultimate in freestyle cooking. Glance through the recipes and alternative suggestions and you will find that your own ideas start to appear. Scrawl them down or, better still, paint a large piece of MDF or hardboard with blackboard paint and hang it up in the kitchen for your personal eureka moments.

- *You can add but you can't take away.* Perhaps the most important mantra for non-recipe cooking. Print this out in huge capital letters and put it on the kitchen wall!

- Taste as you go along and adjust accordingly. Your palette is a far better guide for ingredient quantities than a recipe. Start trusting in your taste buds and they won't let you down.

- When you want to combine a set of ingredients, begin with the ingredient you think you've got the least of. That way you'll have a chance to adjust the flavouring if you don't manage to generate enough taste from a scarce ingredient.

- Cut, chop or slice all your ingredients before beginning to cook and combine. In their prepared state you'll get a much better idea of how much to add or not. Don't worry if you chopped or sliced stuff you can't use in that particular recipe. That's where your selection of plastic containers comes in.

- Embrace the concept of *substitution of ingredients*. Before you leg it down to the nearest supermarket to get more stuff, ask yourself, "Have I got anything I can use instead?" So when a recipe asks for ground coriander and you only have cumin, does it really matter? Probably not. My non-pesto recipe on page 130 is a perfect illustration of this, substituting the traditional pesto ingredients with more everyday ingredients to create an alternative pesto.

- As a rule of thumb, use robust herbs, such as rosemary, sage and thyme, for meat dishes and add them at the start of cooking. Use fragile herbs, such as chives, chervil, dill and flat leaf parsley, for fish and include them at the very end of cooking. The essential oils and flavour of fragile herbs dissipate quickly with heat, so add them when you've removed the pan from the heat source just prior to serving. If you're using dried herbs, use half the quantity of fresh.

Chopping your ingredients before you begin will help you judge how much to add.

Re-heating cooked food

Using cooked food that's been kept in the fridge and then re-heated is a major means of reducing waste. Embrace this idea alone and you will see your food waste plummet and cash increase. Cooking puts a stop to the enzyme activity that contributes to the general discolouration and deterioration of vegetables. Once cooked, covered and refrigerated or frozen, further decay is slowed down dramatically. A 180°C (Gas Mark 4) preheated oven is the optimum for heating up previously cooked and chilled food.

One of the things I've learnt through talking to people on my cooking-demonstration travels is that most of us are trapped in the idea that preparing and serving meals is a once-only occurrence. This is exacerbated by an endemic fear of re-heating cooked food, particularly meat, pasta and rice – though you do need to be careful with cooked rice (see page 123). Given the plethora of ready-cooked meals that populate supermarket shelves, from the humble cottage pie to entire Indian banquets, all waiting to be rejuvenated with a quick blast of the microwave, this fear of heating up home-cooked food seems a tad unnecessary. Or maybe it explains it? Perhaps we see these ready-cooked meals – a phenomenon of the last 20 years – as being created by scientists under laboratory conditions in order to magically render them safe for re-heating. Undoubtedly they are created under conditions as sterile as a surgeon's theatre, but by following a few simple guidelines for cooling and refrigerating, virtually any cooked food can be re-heated for safe consumption without any deterioration in flavour.

The secret is to cool the food down as quickly as possible (but not in the fridge or freezer as hot food will raise the fridge temperature). This is best achieved by spreading it out in a thin layer on a shallow tray or plate to enable quick and even

Those roast dinner leftovers taste just as good re-heated.

cooling. Always remember that residual heat will continue cooking food after it has been removed from the heat source. As soon as the food reaches room temperature, put it into a plastic container, cover and refrigerate. Fish is the only thing I wouldn't re-heat, with exception of fishcakes and fish pie. Not because there's any danger, but because fish cooks so quickly, there's no real need for advance cooking. Also, unlike meat and vegetables, fish has an inherent delicacy and so re-heating tends to spoil the finished dish.

By following a few simple guidelines for cooling and refrigerating, virtually any cooked food can be re-heated for safe consumption without any deterioration in flavour.

Cook-and-chill and par-cooking

Whether you're entertaining a small army of people with aspirations of haute cuisine, or rustling up a bit of scram for your tea, the cook-and-chill technique will save you time and waste. Cooking tired old vegetables not only puts a hold on further food deterioration but also gives you loads of pre-cooked food for your fridge or freezer. Then all you need to do is re-heat it. And this in no way detracts from the final dish – if anything, it often makes it tastier than ever. This handy technique will give you the inspiration and the means to create delicious dishes in the blink of an eye. For recipes that specialise in pre-cooked veg, see Cooked leftovers (pages 138-147).

Pre-cooking green veg (cabbage, beans and peas) Green veg such as green beans can be cooked in salted water then refreshed under cold water (to stop the cooking process and bring out the vibrant colour) before being refrigerated for later use. Prepared in this way, they should last for up to a week in the fridge. To serve, simply heat a knob of butter and a tablespoon of water in a pan, add the beans, some freshly ground black pepper and sea salt, and in a couple of minutes the water will have reduced, leaving a glorious shiny glaze to your piping hot beans. Hey presto - you've got restaurant-style veg in minutes.

---

*Par-cooking doesn't half make life easier.
And it does away with that timing panic
in the face of expectant guests.*

Par-cooking

Par-cooking is a standard restaurant technique that I find surprisingly absent from most cookbooks. But it doesn't half make life easier, and generally does away with that head-scrambling, manic-panic stage of 'timing everything so it's all ready at the same time'. Essentially it involves taking food prep one step away from being finished, allowing the food to cool then storing it in the appropriate fashion until required.

For example, this may involve cooking a risotto until al dente (with a firm bite), cooling it down as quickly as possible then refrigerating until required. To serve, just heat it in a pan with an extra ladle of stock then stir in your other pre-prepared ingredients, such as cooked mushrooms, butternut squash purée and grated Parmesan. It's ready in no time – plus you don't have the worry of messing it up in front of expectant guests because you got the hard bit over with the day before (so if you did mess up, you had plenty of time to try again).

This technique is particularly useful when serving a full English breakfast for a house full of guests. Simply cook each ingredient to the point where a few minutes of further grilling or oven heat would render them ready, then set aside. Even poached eggs can be par-cooked. Simmer them in water with a splash of white wine vinegar until firm enough to remove with a slotted spoon without falling apart, then plunge them straight into iced water. You can even store them in the fridge like this overnight. When they're required, lower them into a pan of fresh, very hot water to warm through – this will also firm up the white.

The scary cupboard

Exploring the underworld of the expired 'best before' date gives you one of your greatest weapons in the war on waste and can result in a veritable treasure trove of magnificent, practically free flavours for marinades, rubs and sauces. I came up with the term 'scary cupboard' while talking to a bunch of students from Coventry University about food waste. It's the culinary equivalent of your gran's old cellar that used to scare you as a kid – think black-and-white horror movie with moody orchestral soundtrack and you'll be right back there.

I am, of course, referring to that above-the-treeline cupboard containing all those dried herbs, spices, strange oils and vinegars that you were given as gifts. Or perhaps you purchased them some years ago in a bid to recreate that memorable dish you sampled in the home of the village chief during a gap year on the Yucatán Peninsula. And let me guess – it just didn't taste the same and the ingredients have never seen the light of day since? Let's face it, even if you wanted to take them out of the cupboard, you can't due to the dried layer of dark, unidentifiable superglue-strength gloop anchoring everything permanently to the shelf.

But it doesn't have to be this way, as my Coventry converts will enthusiastically testify. Facing your fears head-on is a sure-fire way to overcome them. Sorting that cupboard and welcoming what it has to offer is a short, sharp pain in return for a life ahead of joyous exploration. Just dive in and fill your boots!

There's often a wealth of flavouring potential piled up at the back of the cupboard.

A strong word on 'best before' and 'use by' dates

What did we do a couple of decades ago when 'best before' or 'use by' dates didn't exist? We used our senses – looking, smelling and even tasting. The 'best before' date is simply a manufacturer's guideline, indicating the date after which the quality of the product can't be guaranteed. Dried herbs and spices gradually lose their intensity of aroma and flavour after that date, so when assessing whether or not to use them, open them up and take in the aroma. If it's starting to diminish, just use a little extra to compensate. They won't make you ill or give you food poisoning. This is where trusting your senses will save you money and increase your cooking options.

'Use by' dates are more informative. They generally appear on highly perishable protein-based foods such as meat and fish. While I'm not advocating ignoring them or using produce after that date, a fridge maintained at a temperature of 1°C will offer greater life than a fridge at, say, 5°C. I keep my fridge as cold as it can be without freezing. As a result, my milk is still in perfect condition some seven days after the label has told me to bin it. The same goes for cream and cheese. When it comes to meat and fish, don't take any chances unless you are 100-per-cent certain. Now and again I will use some meat or fish a couple of days after the 'use by' date, but my fridge is extra-cold and I will have given the produce a thorough multi-sensory going-over.

Dealing with mistakes

Whether you're a culinary magician or an ingredients-challenged, microwave-crazy numpty, things go wrong in kitchens. The secret is to keep your head and turn disaster into glory. Tears and tantrums may be knee-jerk reactions but won't help. And just remember, some of the world's greatest recipes were spawned from the remnants of things gone wrong. In fact, as you master the techniques of non-recipe cooking, handling things that don't go to plan is a fundamental part of the learning process and will add to your repertoire and skills.

Things can go wrong for even the best of chefs . . .

Rescue remedies

My plan was to create a watercress sauce to have with a fillet of seared salmon. The first thing that went wrong was that I broke my kitchen mantra, *You can add but you can't take away*. Being somewhat over-hungry after a rare foray into the gym, I added too much stock to the leaves and wound up with soup rather than sauce. A rescue plan of adding crème fraîche and cornflour to thicken in order to get back my sauce consistency produced mistake number two: I took my eye off the ball and spilt the crème fraîche. My revamped sauce now resembled some alien glob and really did look unsalvageable. But I needed to eat – and quickly! My next course of action? A quick sieve of the soupy sauce took out the little white floaters, while a rummage in the scary cupboard dug up some two-year-old udon noodles (I know – what the heck!). I dumped the noodles into the soup and heated them for a few minutes, then sliced the salmon and chucked it in, followed by the surviving leaves of some coriander stored in kitchen paper and cling film (more on this on page 98). The result: some top-dinner tucker – but not before I rattled off a few pics for your benefit.

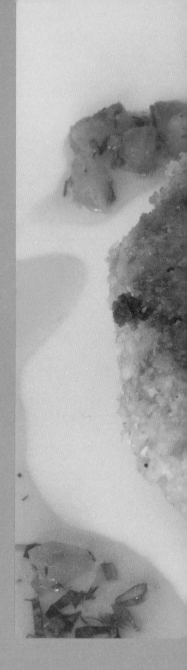

The recipes

OK, enough of the theory – time to tantalise the taste buds. Just remember that the majority of these recipes are simply guidelines and suggestions for you to interpret and adapt according to your own taste and ingredients. Very soon you will be relishing your own brand of ultimate freestyle cooking.

Eggs (and butter, milk, cream and flour)

I've grouped these ingredients under the same heading simply because they're so often used in conjunction with each other. With this little list of staples you will never be short of a tasty meal or a vessel for leftovers in the form of Yorkshire puddings, pancakes or a flavoursome flan. Making shortcrust pastry is incredibly easy, and it can be given a gourmet twist with the simple addition of herbs, roasted garlic, lemon zest, vanilla, and so on. I've also included a couple of standard sauces, which can be combined with or accompany all kinds of cooked veg, meat, fish and cupboard basics. With these ingredients you could bake almost any bread, cake and pastry you desire, but my aim is to use them in quick and practical ways, *Ready Steady Cook* style.

The humble chicken's egg is outrageously underrated, yet it's perhaps one of nature's most remarkable gifts to the foodie world; a chef's dream creation. The runny yolk of a perfectly poached egg, trickling over freshly steamed asparagus, is a ready-made sauce that the greatest culinary minds in the world could never have contrived. The egg is one of our best weapons in the war on food waste, as it congeals and combines with just about anything thrown at it: tired vegetable offcuts or wilted herbs are transformed into a mouth-watering omelette; a crumbled morsel of black pudding or grease-coated bit of bacon effortlessly morph into *oeuf en cocotte*; and an eye-infested old potato and a few slices of onion become a

sublime Spanish tortilla. Egg yolks can be used to make creamy carbonaras or a quick hollandaise, egg whites can be whisked and mixed into a light, fluffy soufflé (not half as difficult as you think), and then there's the endless array of brownies, cakes and tarts. Give me an egg, and I'll show you a meal.

On a health note, eggs were once considered to be high in bad cholesterol. Not so now. Apparently, they contain good cholesterol, so after all those years of two a week, I'm now making up for lost time at the rate of two a day!

Storing eggs and dairy

Bear in mind that the 'best before' date on eggs relates to them being stored at room temperature. They will be good for at least another four or five weeks if stored in the fridge, but even then, don't consign an egg to the bin until you've cracked it open – you'll know if it's off by the smell! There's also the old freshness test that involves submerging an egg into a bowl of water. A fresh egg should sit firmly at the bottom on its side, while a bad egg will float to the surface. The freshest eggs are best for poaching, as the white stays clinging to the yolk rather than dissipating into stringy clouds, and slightly older eggs are good for scrambling and omelettes. Where just egg yolks are required for recipes such as hollandaise sauce (page 45), you can freeze the egg whites (label the container with the date). Remember that, for most cooking purposes, eggs are better used at room temperature.

A good, super-cold fridge will have a considerable positive effect on the actual life of your milk, cream and crème fraîche, as opposed to the 'use by' date, but let your senses be the judge of their relative freshness!

Yorkshire puddings

These little puds are the best edible vessel for random leftovers. They freeze beautifully, and can be taken straight out of the freezer, filled with fridge-cold leftovers and put in the oven for about 15 minutes – by which time both puddings and contents will be heated through. And you don't even need a set of scales.

Makes about 24 mini Yorkshire puddings

1 mug plain flour
pinch of salt
1 mug eggs (3-4 eggs), beaten
1 mug milk
vegetable oil

You will also need: whisk; muffin tin

Put the flour and seasoning into a bowl, make a well and add the eggs. Pour in a little milk and start to whisk (ideally with an electric whisk). Gradually add the rest of the milk until you have a smooth batter.

Cover the mixture and refrigerate for at least 30 minutes before using. You can even make it a day in advance, but be sure to give it a good stir or whisk before using. Preheat the oven to 220°C (Gas Mark 7).

Put a Yorkshire pudding tray or muffin tin in the oven for 5-10 minutes, then remove it and pour a thin film of vegetable oil into the bottom of each recess.

Return the tray or tin to the oven for 2 minutes to get it really hot – almost smoking. Remove it again, pour the batter mixture up to the rim in each recess, then carefully put back into the oven.

Cook for about 20 minutes, or until the puddings have risen and are brown and crispy around the top. (Resist the temptation to keep opening the oven door to check them, as this will prevent a good rise.)

Five gourmet Yorkshire pudding fillings

★ Leftover roast chicken dinner - just chop, combine and add
★ Roast beef, horseradish cream and watercress
★ Cheesy roast garlic mushrooms (page 85)
★ Sausage, courgettes and peas in tomato sauce (page 145)
★ Bubble and squeak (page 147)

Pancakes

This is another fantastically freezable, edible wrap for all kinds of stuff you just wouldn't think of. If you are freezing them, separate each pancake with a piece of greaseproof paper and then wrap in foil or cling film.

Makes around 12 pancakes

125g plain flour
pinch of salt
3 eggs
250ml milk
oil for frying

Put the flour and salt into a bowl, make a well and add the eggs. Gradually whisk in the milk until you have a smooth batter.

Heat a non-stick frying pan and carefully apply a very thin film of oil using a bundle of kitchen paper. Pour in a ladle of batter and quickly tip the pan around from side to side to get a thin, even layer of batter.

When the pancake is golden brown on the underside, turn it over and cook the other side for another 30 seconds. Tip the pancake out on to a plate and repeat the process.

Four tempting pancake fillings

★ Shredded creamed cabbage with Cheddar and pancetta (page 75)
★ Cheesy roast garlic mushrooms (page 85)
★ Sausage, courgettes and peas in tomato sauce (page 145)
★ Poached fruit and whipped cream (see stock syrup recipe, page 150)

Pot Noodle pancakes

Don't forget, you saw it here first! After consulting a group of students about their common cupboard ingredients (yes, the clue is in the title), I had my quintessential Heston moment. And by George it worked a treat. Now the Pot Noodle purists among you may wonder why I would mess with such a flawless creation, but I discovered that the dried pot contents offer a very flavoursome flour substitute. Not only does this remarkable reworking create a good old-fashioned pancake, but its taste and pliable texture also pack such a punch that it reminds me of a classic Ethiopian or Eritrean flatbread – perfect for tearing and sharing and scooping up the remnants of last night's curry. You really have to try it to believe it!

Makes 6 x 20cm pancakes

1 Pot Noodle
200ml milk
3 eggs

You will also need: stick blender with bowl attachment or food processor

Remove the soy sauce sachet from the noodle pot and set aside. Blend the remaining dried Pot Noodle contents using a stick blender with bowl attachment or food processor until powdered, then pour into a bowl.

Add the contents of the soy sachet, the milk and the eggs. Whisk to a smooth batter (it won't be as smooth as if you'd used flour, but don't worry, it doesn't affect the result) and then follow the pancake recipe opposite.

Egg, anchovy and roast pepper bruschetta

Scrambled eggs is another one of those recipes that's just begging for the addition of exciting flavours. Chorizo, smoked salmon and cheese are among the more traditional choices, but this little combo, inspired by a Spanish tapas recipe, illustrates the many variations at your disposal. I reckon tinned tuna, spring onions or a handful of prawns would work equally well. I'm sure you can think of loads more ideas.

Makes 10 bruschetta

1 baguette, cut into 10 slices, 2cm thick
olive oil for brushing
14 anchovies in oil, cut lengthways down the middle
1 roasted red pepper (page 94), skinned, deseeded and sliced
4 eggs, beaten
seasoning to taste

To garnish:
half a green pepper, thinly sliced into 20 pieces and gently fried for 2 minutes

Brush the baguette slices with olive oil. Heat a griddle pan and cook the slices on each side for about 2 minutes until nicely marked with the griddle bars. Alternatively, bake the slices in a preheated oven at 180°C (Gas Mark 4) for a few minutes until lightly coloured, or grill or toast.

Heat the anchovies and slices of red pepper in a saucepan, add the beaten eggs and scramble. You can add black pepper, but go easy on the salt due to the salty nature of the anchovies.

Heap on to the cooked baguette slices and cross each one with two slices of green pepper.

Whatever-you-want flan

This recipe includes courgettes for the filling simply because that's what I needed to use up at the time of cooking and writing, but you could also use cheese, bacon, broccoli, salmon or sausage, etc. Really any pre-cooked ingredients you fancy can go into the filling – the only restriction is your imagination. All you need to remember for your base recipe is half fat to flour for the pastry, and 285ml cream to 3 eggs for the filling. After that it's a case of, in the immortal words of Status Quo, "Whatever you want"!

Serves 4

For the pastry:
200g plain flour, plus extra for dusting
½ tsp salt
100g diced butter, slightly softened at room temperature, plus extra for greasing
a little under 50ml water
zest of 1 lemon (optional)

For the filling:
3 eggs, beaten
4 chargrilled courgette strips (page 81)
285ml cream
seasoning

You will also need: food processor (not crucial but useful); tart tin; dried beans

First, make the pastry. Combine all the pastry ingredients in a food processor for a few seconds. Turn the mixture out on to a lightly floured work surface and gather into a smooth ball of dough. Wrap tightly in cling film and rest in the fridge for 30 minutes. Preheat the oven to 180°C (Gas Mark 4).

If you don't have a food processor, sift the flour and salt into a bowl then add the butter. Work the butter into the flour quickly and lightly using your fingertips until the mixture resembles breadcrumbs.

Add the water and lemon zest (if using) and form into a smooth dough.

While the dough is resting, make the filling. Combine the beaten eggs with the rest of the filling ingredients and set aside.

Remove the pastry dough from the fridge. Roll it out on a lightly floured work surface to about 3mm thick and carefully put it into a lightly buttered tart tin. Using a small floured piece of pastry dough, press the pastry lightly into the tin, leaving an

overhang. Line the base with a circle of baking parchment then fill it with dried beans. Place in the oven and bake blind (i.e. without the filling) for 10 minutes.

Remove the beans and parchment and return to the oven for a further 5 minutes to cook the base.

Remove from the oven. Give the filling mixture a good stir then carefully pour it into the pastry case. Bake for about 25 minutes, or until golden brown.

Take out of the oven, allow to cool, trim the pastry edges and then serve – or eat freshly baked from the oven . . .

Perfect omelette

One of my top five quick lunches. Apart from the exquisite taste and texture of a well-executed omelette, it's a fantastic fold-over vessel for an assortment of leftovers. Serve with a warm potato salad (page 90) or roast new potatoes (page 88) and green veg or composite salad (page 131). So for the base omelette, forget any other ingredient – apart from salt and pepper – and stick to the main player. I reckon three eggs are what you need for a decent individual serving. A timing tip: make sure you prepare and portion all your filling ingredients in advance.

Makes 1 omelette

3 eggs
seasoning
butter or oil for frying

Put your non-stick frying pan over a high heat without adding any cooking fat. Meanwhile, beat the eggs with a fork and season with salt and pepper.

After 2 minutes, add a knob of butter or the slightest drizzle of oil, immediately followed by the beaten egg. Start to agitate the pan and simultaneously stir the egg vigorously (a bit like patting head and rubbing stomach at the same time). At this point, everything should be taking place in a hazy blur of hand movements.

While there's still a runny film of unset egg on the surface of the omelette, take it off the heat and add a bit of whatever you fancy.

Quickly fold over the omelette and slide it on to your plate.

Five omelette fillings

★ Fresh fine herbs (random selection of finely chopped parsley, dill, chervil, chives)
★ Grated cheese and tinned tuna
★ Smoked haddock
★ Shredded creamed cabbage with Cheddar and pancetta (see page 75)
★ Spag bol – pasta and all! (see page 146)

Baked eggs

This recipe simply involves baking an egg in a buttered ramekin dish, with random cooked bits in the base and a dollop of double cream and seasoning on top. What you put in the base is entirely down to what you fancy and what you have. After a few minutes' baking in a little warm water bath, the result is a luxury breakfast to satisfy the most indulgent Sunday morning. Serve with hot buttered toast soldiers for dipping.

Makes 2 baked eggs

oil for frying
1 heaped tbsp bacon bits or pancetta cubes
3-5 button mushrooms, sliced
½ tsp chopped fresh thyme
seasoning to taste
butter for greasing
2 eggs
2 tbsp double cream

You will also need: 2 ramekin dishes

Preheat the oven to 180°C (Gas Mark 4).

Heat a little oil in a frying pan over a high heat and fry the bacon or pancetta cubes until lightly browned. Remove from the pan and set aside.

Add the mushrooms, thyme and a little seasoning to the pan. Fry for 2 minutes then add the bacon.

Lightly butter the ramekin dishes and divide the mushroom and bacon mixture between them. Carefully break an egg into each one, then spoon over a tablespoon of cream and season. Place the ramekins in an ovenproof dish or baking tin, boil the kettle and add enough hot water to come about halfway up the ramekins. Bake in the preheated oven for about 15 minutes, or until the eggs are just set.

White sauce

Otherwise known as béchamel, white sauce is a mix of flour, butter and milk. However, you could add a few parsley stalks, a bay leaf and/or a segment of onion (preferably studded with cloves) to the milk at the beginning of cooking. If left to infuse for a few minutes before straining, it will make a huge difference to the taste of the finished sauce. Pretty much anything can be added to this creamy, smooth-as-silk sauce, including cheese, fried bacon and sautéd mushrooms. To make the béchamel into a tasty cheese sauce, stir in a good handful of grated Cheddar until you get your desired level of cheesiness.

Serves 4 as an accompanying sauce

50g butter
50g plain flour
450ml milk
seasoning

Optional:
couple of sprigs of flat leaf parsley
1 bay leaf
half an onion, pierced with 2 cloves

Melt the butter in a small non-stick pan over a medium heat then stir in the flour. Cook and stir for 2 minutes then set aside.

Heat the milk in a saucepan with the parsley, bay leaf and onion (if using). Just as the milk comes to a simmer, remove from the heat and leave to stand for 10 minutes before straining.

Return the pan with the butter and flour to a low heat. Start adding the strained milk a little at a time, making sure you stir until smooth before adding the next bit of milk. (The mixture will be very thick to begin with, but don't worry, it will quickly thin out as you add more milk.) Meanwhile, taste and add seasoning.

Once fully combined, remove from the heat. If you're not using the sauce straight away, transfer it to a plastic container, put a piece of cling film over the surface of the sauce to prevent a skin from forming and store in the fridge.

Hollandaise sauce

Another straightforward sublime sauce. Of course, you could go through the rigmarole of reducing white wine and white wine vinegar with finely diced shallots, parsley stalks and peppercorns for a restaurant-style version, or you can forget that and follow this simple recipe for a superb and authentic result. Once the sauce is made you do need to serve it soon, so best to cover the bowl with cling film and leave it in a warm place.

Serves 2 as an accompanying sauce

125g butter
1 egg yolk
1 tsp white wine vinegar
juice of half a lemon
seasoning

Melt the butter in a saucepan over a low to medium heat, or in the microwave.

Set a bowl over a pan of gently simmering water and put the egg yolk in the bowl along with the vinegar, lemon juice and seasoning. Whisk until the mix becomes pale and thick.

Remove from the heat, place the bowl on a tea towel or damp cloth so it doesn't slip, and start whisking in the warm melted butter. Start with a few drops at a time to create an emulsion, then add the butter in a steady stream, whisking continuously, until the mixture is thick and fully combined.

For other recipe ideas for eggs, see:

Spanish tortilla (page 92)
Spag bol revisited: four uses for two tablespoons of spag bol (in an omelette) (page 146)

Cheese

Cheese, glorious cheese! Where would we be without it? Cheese on toast is perhaps one of our earliest culinary memories. And while I will devour an entire baked Camembert studded with rosemary and garlic then pasted on to lightly toasted baguette, equally I will drool over chunks of processed Edam plonked into a piping-hot bowl of tinned tomato soup to produce spiderweb-like strands of cheese.

Given our partiality for this dairy stalwart, it's surprising that it gets consigned to the bin with such wanton regularity. Perhaps it is down to our over-zealous health-and-safety culture, or because cheese is one of the first victims of that green mouldy bloom. There are few dishes that I think wouldn't benefit from the addition of some type of cheese, so there's really no excuse for not using it before it walks out of the fridge of its own accord.

The key to maximising the shelf life of your cheese is storage – always in the fridge. Hard cheeses like Parmesan will last almost indefinitely and are fine wrapped in cling film. Medium-hard cheeses such as Cheddar are also fine in cling film and kept in an airtight container. If these cheeses form an external green mould, just cut it off, slicing an outer centimetre to make sure you get rid of it all. Soft cheeses such as Brie and Camembert have the shortest shelf lives and are best stored wrapped in baking parchment then cling film and kept in an airtight container.

Pan-fried goats' cheese salad with spiced nuts

This is a fabulous way to add a gourmet touch to a slice of ordinary goats' cheese, while using up leftover frozen brioche from some long-gone pâté dish. Brioche makes amazing breadcrumbs, giving a subtle sweetness and crunchy texture. A ferret around in the scary cupboard should turn up some old nuts. Pecans are ideal, but the concept will work brilliantly with any kind of nuts.

Serves 2

For the spiced nuts:
1 tbsp olive, groundnut or rapeseed oil
90g pecan or mixed nuts of your choice
¼ tsp cayenne pepper
½ tsp cinnamon
1 tsp Worcester sauce
a few drops of Tabasco sauce

For the goats' cheese:
1 tbsp plain flour, lightly seasoned
2 eggs, beaten
70g brioche bread, blitzed with a stick blender to form breadcrumbs
2 x 100g discs of goats' cheese log

For the salad:
2 large handfuls of mixed-leaf salad
1 tbsp salad dressing of your choice

To serve: 2 tbsp oil for frying

Preheat the oven to 180°C (Gas Mark 4).

First, make the spiced nuts. Heat the oil in a frying pan then add all the spiced nut ingredients. Stir and toss the mixture for 3-4 minutes until the nuts are well coated. Remove from the heat and set aside to cool.

To prepare the goats' cheese, place the seasoned flour in one bowl, the beaten eggs in another and the brioche breadcrumbs in a third. Carefully dip each disc of cheese first in the flour, patting off any excess, then in the egg and finally in the brioche breadcrumbs. Add one more coat of egg wash and breadcrumbs, then set aside or store in an airtight container in the fridge.

To serve, heat 2 tbsp of oil in a frying pan over a moderate heat and fry the cheese for 2 minutes on each side until lightly golden. Place on a baking tray and transfer to the oven for about 10 minutes.

Toss the salad and a few of the nuts in the dressing just before serving and then arrange on a plate with the goats' cheese and the remaining nuts.

Welsh rarebit

Thank you, Gary Rhodes! I've made umpteen Welsh rarebit recipes over the years, but not one has come close to Gary's recipe in his awesome *New British Classics* cookbook. Simple and brilliant, it ticks all the rarebit boxes – mouth-wateringly melting and perfectly piquant. Moreover, it will freeze well. It's got wonderful versatility – spread it on toast, grill and cut into soldiers for your boiled egg or, for a bit of dinner-party luxury, serve on top of a smoked haddock fillet.

350g Cheddar, grated
85ml milk
25g plain flour
25g fresh white breadcrumbs
½ tbsp English mustard powder
a few drops of Worcester sauce
seasoning
1 egg
1 egg yolk

Put the Cheddar and the milk in a heavy-based pan over a low heat and gradually melt the cheese. Do not allow to boil.

When the cheese has melted and the mixture is smooth, add the flour, bread-crumbs and mustard.

Cook for a few minutes over a low heat until the mixture comes together away from the pan sides. Add the Worcester sauce and seasoning and leave until cooled to room temperature.

Add the egg and egg yolk and beat in until fully combined. Chill the mixture in the fridge before using.

Four Welsh rarebit meals

* Filo balls: form the cold rarebit mix into balls, wrap in 2 layers of buttered filo pastry and deep-fry.
* Grilled on toast and topped with soft-boiled or fried egg and bacon.
* With smoked haddock: spread on top of the uncooked smoked haddock and bake for 15 minutes.
* Crostini (page 54): just spread on and grill for 2 minutes.

Cheesy profiteroles

Mention pastry to most cooks and it's quite likely to induce a cold sweat. If you're talking about filo or puff pastry, that's totally understandable, but choux is so simple you could get the kids to do it. You can substitute beer for the water, but who has leftover beer? (Well, apparently 3,000 unopened cans or bottles of it get binned every day by us at home! 'Best before' dates have a lot to answer for.) For an extra bit of luxury, pipe in the kidney bean and blue cheese dip on page 137.

Makes about 20 bite-sized balls

125ml water
30g butter, plus extra for greasing
75g plain flour
pinch of salt
2 eggs
30g Cheddar, grated

Preheat the oven to 180°C (Gas Mark 4).

Heat the water in a pan, add the butter and melt. Add the flour and salt and beat until the mixture forms into a smooth ball.

Remove from the heat, add 1 egg and beat until combined. Add the second egg and mix again. The mixture should be smooth and shiny.

Using a teaspoon or dessertspoon, depending on how big you want the finished profiteroles, spoon the mixture on to a buttered baking tray and place at the top of the oven for 10 minutes, or until the profiteroles are golden brown and crispy on top.

Open the oven door and leave for another 10 minutes. The profiteroles can now be filled with a filling of your choice. Try the cheesy potato garlic dip on page 89.

For other recipe ideas for cheese, see:

Whatever-you-want flan (page 40)
Perfect omelette: five omelette fillings (grated cheese and tinned tuna) (page 42)
White sauce (page 44)
Butternut squash and goats' cheese risotto (page 73)
Cauliflower (page 79)
Cheese and tuna pasta: three key pasta sauces (cream-based sauce) (page 121)
Braised celery with Stilton and walnut crust (page 129)
Hey pesto (page 130)
Kidney bean and blue cheese dip (page 137)

Bread

Did you know that we, in the UK, throw away approximately 37 million slices – 2 million loaves – of bread a *day*?* That's a lot of bread, folks. Personally I keep my sliced bread in the freezer and take out what I need when I need it. It defrosts in minutes without a microwave, and can be put straight into the toaster or under the grill from frozen. French sticks or baguettes are never the same the day after purchase. However, sliced into thin little pieces, doused with olive oil and sprinkled with seasoning, they make the most delectable dipping utensils (see crostini, page 54) and savoury platforms for all manner of leftovers. And with the prospect of breadcrumbs, puddings and my special instant mini bread tart cases (page 56), you'll never need to throw away bread again.

* From 'Household food and drink waste in the UK, November 2009', WRAP

> 🍲 **Perfect breadcrumbs** For the best breadcrumbs, use bread that's been left out for about 24 hours. Having said that, fresh bread blitzed in a food processor or bread that's completely stale and dried out will work out equally well. Breadcrumbs are best stored in an airtight container in a cool, dry place or frozen in takeaway containers. You can use them practically straight out of the freezer.

Chilli and cheese breadcrumbs

Uses: leftover bread, oil, cheese, chilli flakes, dried herbs, spices

You can use the trimmings from the mini bread tart cases on page 56, or use fresh or stale leftover bread. These breadcrumbs are fabulous sprinkled over broccoli then baked. They also make an ideal base for savoury cheesecake (page 72) or a tasty snack to munch on instead of crisps and nuts. Simply spread the trimmings on a baking tray, drizzle with oil, grate liberally with cheese and sprinkle over chilli flakes, dried herbs, or any herbs and spices of your choice. Bake for several minutes until golden brown. Allow to cool then pulse into breadcrumbs with a stick blender or in a food processor. Store in an airtight container in a cool dry place.

Crostini

Uses: baguettes, olive oil, seasoning

Crostini are the incredible result of baking baguettes – fresh or stale – in the oven for a few minutes. They make a simple but scrumptious base for all manner of leftovers, which can be served as canapés, and they're perfect for dipping too. Preheat the oven to 180°C (Gas Mark 4). Slice the baguette into ½cm slices and arrange in a single layer on a baking tray. Drizzle over olive oil and sprinkle with sea salt and freshly ground black pepper. Place in the preheated oven until lightly golden around the edges then allow to cool. They can be stored in an airtight container in a cool, dry place (not the fridge) for days. Try spreading a few with Welsh rarebit (page 49) then stick them under the grill for 2-3 minutes for amazing party nibbles or midnight munchies.

Flatbread

With all those alien ingredients and variables like yeast, which necessitates
'proving' and 'knocking back', you'd be right to steer clear of such as a scary recipe
as bread. That's why I've done away with the aforementioned and now declare
"bread in under five minutes" at my live shows. It doesn't half grab people's
attention! Furthermore, you can totally customise the recipe using all manner of
ingredients. The only essentials are flour, water and salt. After that, throw in
anything from out-of-date dried herbs to sun-dried tomatoes. Personally, I like the
combination of lemon zest, roast garlic and fresh thyme. Or try the version below,
with sausage and roast garlic.

Makes 4 flatbreads

200g plain flour, plus extra for dusting
100ml water
1 tsp salt
half a roast garlic bulb (see page 83)
1 cooked sausage, finely chopped
zest of 1 lemon
oil for frying

Combine all the ingredients in a bowl to
form a smooth dough. Divide into 4 pieces
and roll out to a few millimetres thick on a
floured surface. You can freeze the
flatbreads between sheets of baking
parchment.

To cook, pan-fry in a little oil over a
medium–high heat for a few minutes on
each side until golden brown, or put
straight on to a griddle pan or barbecue.

Mini bread tart cases

One of my guilty pleasures is ultra-processed sliced white bread with a couple of Dairylea cheese triangles spread out in the middle. Luckily it also makes great breadcrumbs and is ideal for this pastry-substitute tart case recipe. This is simply the tart case version of the crostini and makes the perfect vessel for turning leftover cooked food into moreish bite-sized canapés. Keep a stack of cases to hand, and every time you've got leftover cooked food, chop it up, put it in the tart cases and freeze. Try them with remnants of leftover spag bol then warm through in the oven (see page 146).

Makes 12 tart cases

6 slices white bread, with crusts removed for making into chilli and cheese breadcrumbs (page 54)
oil for brushing

dried herbs (optional)
seasoning

You will also need: 12-cup muffin tin (or a 6-cup one – just do 2 batches); round cutter (1cm wider than the muffin cups)

Preheat the oven to 180°C (Gas Mark 4).

Use a rolling pin to roll out each bread slice. Cut out 2 discs from each slice using the cutter. Set the trimmings aside with the crusts.

Brush the muffin cups lightly with oil and press a bread disc into each cup. Brush lightly with oil, add a scattering of herbs (if using) and season with salt and pepper.

Bake the bread tart cases in the oven for about 7 minutes, or until lightly brown around the edges. Remove and cool. Store in an airtight container in a cool, dry place (not the fridge).

Instant croissant trifle

The look and taste of this 'instant trifle' defies its low cost and simplicity of prep. The stock syrup transforms stale croissants or panettone into tasty sponge, and converts under-ripe fruit into sweet and juicy, melt-in-the-mouth morsels (see page 150). It can be infused with all sorts of flavourings, while the nectarine can be substituted with any fruits you fancy.

Serves 2

Stock syrup:
1 mug water
1 mug caster sugar
1 star anise
1 cinnamon stick
handful of sultanas
1 under-ripe nectarine
1 stale croissant
handful of raspberries
1 dsp icing sugar
1 small tub crème fraîche

To garnish:
1 tbsp mixed nuts, pulsed to chunky crumbs in a food processor

You will also need: stick blender with bowl attachment; 2 large wine glasses to serve

To make the syrup, dissolve the water and sugar in a small saucepan over a gentle heat. Add the star anise, cinnamon stick, sultanas and nectarine, and simmer gently for about 15 minutes. If the nectarine is already ripe, 5 minutes is ample time.

Tear up the croissant and divide between the wine glasses, very gently pressing down into the bottom.

Use a stick blender with bowl attachment to blitz the raspberries with the icing sugar and then combine with the crème fraîche in a bowl – not too much, so you leave pink streaks through the mixture.

To serve, spoon the fruit and a little syrup over each croissant, then top with a dollop of crème fraîche and a sprinkling of nuts.

For other recipe ideas for bread, see:

Hey pesto: four good uses for hey pesto (hey pesto canapés and hey pesto dip – (crostini/flatbread) (page 130)
Composite salads: ideas for composite salads (crostini) (page 131)

The veg rack

Aarggh! The dreaded veg rack! What seems like another brilliant idea as you trip around the supermarket, determined to achieve that elusive haven of health, turns to a pile of greenish sludge as you carry out yet another veg-rack cull. How many more times do you have to groan with pain and remorse before things change?

I've devoted quite a large section of this book to the vegetable rack, not because I sway towards a veggie diet but because veg offers a wonderful opportunity to add fabulous flavour to a whole host of meat and fish dishes, and because it's probably one of the biggest contributory factors to our food waste. For a start, half the stuff you're ditching is probably completely OK and actually at the peak of its flavour. Supermarket fruit and veg are the food equivalent of the human specimens gracing California's Venice Beach – all glossy skin tone, super-enhanced shapes and an ominous absence of wrinkles. Supermarket food culture has conditioned us to believe that fruit and vegetables should look like caricatures of what they actually look like in real life, placing more importance on looks than taste or nutritional content. If you've ever been lucky enough to browse the street markets of France or Italy, you'll have seen that the gnarled, wrinkled and misshapen are revered by those in the know. Also bear in mind that most fruit and veg on the supermarket shelves is harvested under-ripe so as to maximise shelf life and will never achieve optimum flavour.

To achieve veg-rack nirvana, the most crucial point to take on board is that roasting, boiling, frying or chargrilling of the usual suspects will temporarily halt and subsequently slow down the deterioration process. This is a double win, as you will not only reduce waste but also have loads of pre-cooked ingredients which simply need re-heating to provide easy finished meals.

Mixed vegetables

Imagine this dream scenario for a moment. There you are, looking for something to make for dinner, and instead of finding a random selection of decaying veg in the rack, you open the fridge to discover succulent chargrilled courgette strips, roasted red pepper and roasted mushrooms. You boil a pan of pasta and, in the 10 minutes it takes to cook, you re-heat a few spoonfuls of home-made tomato sauce in a saucepan. All you have to do now is quickly chop the veg, warm them through in the sauce for two minutes, pour over the pasta and bingo! A fabulous healthy meal in no time.

Roast veg Roast all your random bits of ageing veg with seasoning, dried herbs and a good slug of oil, and refrigerate and store for longer life and a delicious vegetable base to re-heat.

Roast vegetable tray

Bizarrely, when you roast a whole tray of mixed vegetables – as opposed to boiling, steaming or frying – they all seem to cook at the same rate, melting into one caramelised medley. Once roasted, this concoction becomes the ultimate medium for amazing one-pot meals. It's one of my favourite entertaining base dishes.

The list of ingredients below is purely a guideline. Mix and match in whatever combo you wish. Fennel is wonderful with chicken and fish. Dried herbs such as oregano and mixed herbs (marjoram, basil, oregano and thyme) work as well with fish as they do with meat, while fresh rosemary or thyme make ideal meat accompaniments. The veg can be roasted in advance, cooled down and stored in the fridge for up to five days before re-heating and topping with your choice of meat or fish.

Serves 4 as a vegetable side dish or main dish accompaniment

1 onion
2 carrots
1 celery stick
1 courgette
1 fennel
4 large waxy potatoes
olive or rapeseed oil
dried mixed herbs
seasoning

Preheat the oven to 200°C (Gas Mark 6).

Roughly slice all the veg (not too thin). Spread them out in a roasting tin or an ovenproof dish in as thin a layer as possible and douse them with a good slug of oil.

Sprinkle with the herbs and seasoning then roast for about 40 minutes until the veg are tinged with golden brown edges.

Three fabulous roast vegetable tray meals

★ Shoulder of lamb, marinated in fresh rosemary, lemon zest and anchovies
★ One-pan spatchcocked roast chicken (page 104)
★ Whole baked bream on roasted veg (page 115)

Roast and chargrilled vegetable tart with roast red pepper and tomato sauce

This tart not only makes use of those veg-rack hangers-on but also looks and tastes good enough to serve as a top dinner-party dish. Essentially it's a slightly fancier version of the instant tortilla pizza on page 143, substituting a square of puff pastry for the flour tortilla base along with a slightly more artistic assembly. Don't feel limited to using the vegetables listed here. You can experiment with whatever you have – just think colour and flavour.

Makes 2 tarts

oil for frying
half an onion, sliced thinly
1 dsp tomato purée
2 fresh tomatoes, chopped
½ tin chopped tomatoes
1 garlic clove, crushed (or 1 tsp roast garlic purée – page 83)
1 tsp dried mixed herbs
1 mug vegetable stock
2 slices aubergine, about 1cm thick
olive oil for brushing
seasoning
2 squares ready-rolled puff pastry, about 13 x 13cm
1 roasted red pepper (page 94)
2 baked flat-cap mushrooms (page 84)
4 chargrilled courgette strips (page 81)
cheese for topping

You will also need: stick blender or food processor

Preheat the oven to 180°C (Gas Mark 4).

Add a little oil to a pan and slowly cook the onion over a gentle heat until soft and caramelised. Add the tomato purée and cook for 2 minutes, stirring constantly. Add the fresh and tinned tomatoes, crushed garlic and dried herbs and cook gently for about 10 minutes, until most of the liquid has evaporated. Crush the tomatoes with the back of a spatula if necessary. Remove from the heat.

Now make the filling. Lightly brush the aubergine slices with oil and season with salt and pepper. Heat a griddle pan over a high heat then cook the slices for a few minutes on each side until nicely marked by the griddle bars.

Lightly oil a baking tray and place the pastry squares on top. Put a spoonful of the tomato paste in the middle of each square. Pile up the prepared vegetables, setting aside half the red pepper, and top with the cheese. Bake in the oven until the pastry is puffed up and golden brown, about 20-25 minutes.

While the tarts are baking, make the sauce. Put the remaining tomato paste, the red pepper half and the vegetable stock in a food processor or use a stick blender to blitz to a sauce consistency, adding more water if necessary. Season to taste.

To serve, place each tart in the middle of a dinner plate and spoon around the warmed sauce.

Vegetable tagine

This is the supreme scary-cupboard recipe, and a leap in at the deep end to get to know the inhabitants. On the surface, it's a pretty intimidating list, but the point is, you can chop, change and adapt according to what you have. Chilli flakes can be substituted with Tabasco sauce or chilli powder, dried apricots with prunes, and sultanas with raisins (or leave out altogether). A good grating of lemon zest will help substitute for preserved lemons. The key players for an authentic tagine are really the cumin, ginger, cinnamon and honey, dried fruit and lemon. But, let's face it, with your own blend of spices you've got in the cupboard, it's going to be hard not to achieve a tasty result, regardless of whether you've achieved Moroccan authenticity or not. Serve up with your own version of the couscous recipe on page 125.

Serves 4-6

2 tbsp oil for frying
3-4 onions, thinly sliced
2 carrots, chopped
half a butternut squash, cut into chunks
1 cauliflower, broken into small florets
1 courgette, chopped
1 aubergine, chopped
1 thumb-sized piece of fresh ginger, finely chopped
2 tsp ground coriander
2 tsp ground cumin
1 tsp ground turmeric
½ tsp ground cinnamon
½ tsp chilli flakes
½ tsp all spice
half a roast garlic bulb (page 83)
750ml stock
handful of dried apricots
handful of sultanas
1 tbsp honey
handful of preserved lemons

To garnish:
handful of flaked almonds, lightly toasted in the oven
small bunch of fresh coriander

Heat 1 tbsp oil in a heavy-based pan and add the onions. Cook the onions on a low to medium heat for about 15 minutes.

While the onions are cooking, heat 1 tbsp oil to a frying pan and then fry the veg in separate batches for 2-3 minutes each on a high heat, until they start to go a little brown on the outside. Set aside in their separate piles.

When the onions are cooked, add the ginger and spices, squeeze in the roast garlic and cook for a further 2 minutes, stirring constantly to avoid sticking. Add the stock, give a good stir, then add the carrots. Add the squash and the cauliflower 5 minutes later. When the cauliflower and the carrots are just tender (after about 10 minutes), add all the other ingredients except the almonds and the fresh coriander.

Garnish with the almonds and coriander, and serve with a fantastic-tasting couscous.

Aubergines

Long gone are the days of having to salt aubergines to get rid of their bitterness. The newer Western varieties have got rid of that faff, but not at the expense of flavour so it in no way detracts from the fantastic Middle Eastern dishes you can create with these beautiful specimens. You can cook aubergines in a wide variety of ways, including frying, chargrilling, roasting and even putting them over a naked flame until the skin blackens and is peeled off to reveal soft, smoky flesh with the patina of finest oak.

Baba ganoush

This Middle Eastern classic is a delectable smoky houmous-type dip, but with a truly unique preparation method which involves sticking the whole aubergine straight into an open gas flame. (Unfortunately, electric is no substitute.) This open-flame method gives a fabulous smoked flavour to the flesh. The only downside is the mess it makes of your gas hob, but it will scrub up easily with a little hot water and washing-up liquid.

You may well find a jar of tahini (sesame seed paste) in your scary cupboard, but. if you haven't got any, don't stress too much – the dip will be tasty enough with the remaining ingredients.

2 whole aubergines
2 tsp light tahini
juice of half a lemon
2 small garlic cloves, crushed
4 tsp chopped fresh parsley
seasoning

Place each aubergine directly into an open flame, allowing the skin to blacken and blister before turning. Repeat the process until the whole skin is blackened and blistered, remove from the flame and allow to cool.

Once the flesh has cooled enough to handle, flake off the black skin and drain off any excess liquid in a sieve or colander. Chop up the flesh and combine with the tahini, lemon juice, garlic, fresh parsley and seasoning. Refrigerate until required.

Spicy aubergine pickle

This gorgeous pungent pickle is guaranteed to convert all aubergine sceptics. It's a fabulous condiment in its own right or as part of a meze selection to share or as a tasty topping for bruschetta or as a side dish. But it's when it meets lamb – particularly the spicy variety such as the burgers on page 110 – that it really starts to sing and dance. This is one of those concoctions that tastes much better the next day – after the flavours have had an opportunity to meld together. It should be served at room temperature but stored in an airtight container in the fridge, where it should last for at least three months.

2 aubergines, sliced lengthways into 1cm slices
seasoning
1 dsp olive oil for frying, plus extra for drizzling
1 onion, thinly sliced
1 tbsp fresh ginger, grated (or ½ tbsp ground ginger)
½ tsp chilli powder
½ tsp ground cumin
½ tsp ground turmeric
1 dsp tomato purée
100ml white wine vinegar
1 tbsp honey
1 dsp brown sugar
1 dsp balsamic vinegar
juice of half a lemon

Season the aubergine slices with salt and pepper, and drizzle over a little olive oil.

Heat a griddle pan over a high heat then cook the slices for 2 minutes on each side. Remove, cool, chop into small dice and set aside.

Heat 1 dsp olive oil in a frying pan over a gentle heat and gently sweat the onions until they have softened. Add the ginger and dry spices and cook for 2 minutes, stirring constantly. Add the tomato purée and stir for 1 minute. Add the wine vinegar, honey and sugar and cook for a few minutes until the sugar has dissolved and the liquid has evaporated.

Remove from the heat and immediately add the balsamic vinegar and lemon juice. Finally stir in the diced aubergine. Allow to cool before transferring to an airtight container, then cover and refrigerate.

Stuffed aubergine fritters

These are so good, I managed to demolish an entire plateful kept in the fridge before they'd made it anywhere near the oven for re-heating!

Makes approximately 9 fritters

2 tbsp cream cheese
20g (1 thumb-sized piece) Cheddar, grated
half a roast garlic bulb (page 83)
juice of 1 lemon
1 aubergine, sliced into ½cm discs

4 tbsp plain flour, seasoned
3 eggs, beaten
9 tbsp breadcrumbs
2 tbsp oil for frying

Combine the cream cheese, grated Cheddar, roast garlic purée and lemon juice in a bowl.

Separate the aubergine discs into equally sized pairs. Spoon 1 tsp of the cheese mix on to one disc of each pair, then press on the matching disc to create little aubergine 'sandwiches'.

Place the seasoned flour in one bowl, the egg wash in another bowl and the breadcrumbs in a third. Dust each aubergine pair with the flour before passing through the egg wash and then the breadcrumbs.

Heat the oil in a frying pan over a medium heat then fry the fritters for about 4 minutes on each side, until golden brown and cooked through.

Broccoli
This is one of those supermarket items that elicits a reach-and-grab arm-jerk response. Like it or loathe it, you know you should have it, and before you've even realised, it's in your basket. Fast-forward five days and with heavy heart you consign the whole, still wrapped, brown-edged brassica to the bin.

OK, let's fix this wanton waste. First, just because the florets are tinged with brown doesn't mean the broccoli is done for. A few minutes in boiling water followed by a quick refresh under cold water will temporarily arrest further deterioration and make it look far more appetising. And after a brief re-heat in simmering water, you will have a fine vegetable accompaniment for any occasion. Alternatively, you can bake the whole thing – see the recipe overleaf.

Save the stalks A couple of words on the stalks: they're great. Don't forget that you're buying broccoli by weight, and any stalks that you lop off and bin make up a substantial proportion. So use them don't lose them. Slice them into discs the thickness of a 50p piece and boil them along with the florets. They taste the same and, chopped up or left as they are, make a fabulous addition to salads, pastas, rice dishes and couscous.

Baked broccoli

Broccoli benefits enormously from cooking, cooling and storing, giving you days of happy eating way after you would have had to bin it if left in its raw state.

Serves 4 as a side dish

1 broccoli head, divided into florets
salt
2 tbsp chilli and cheese breadcrumbs (optional – page 54)
olive oil
seasoning
2 tbsp flaked almonds, toasted
Parmesan, grated

Preheat the oven to 180°C (Gas Mark 4).

Put the broccoli florets in a pan of boiling salted water for 2 minutes. Drain well and lay in a single layer in an ovenproof dish. Sprinkle with the breadcrumbs (if using) then liberally douse with olive oil and seasoning. Sprinkle with the almonds and Parmesan and place in the oven for about 25 minutes, or until the broccoli is tender.

For other recipe ideas for broccoli, see:

Whatever-you-want flan (page 40)
Vegetable tagine (page 65)
Hey pesto: four good uses for hey pesto (hey pesto canapés – roasted/chargrilled veg on crostini) (page 130)

Butternut squash

Like broccoli, butternut squash often seems like a great idea in the shop. But once home and staring at it on the chopping board, wondering what on earth to do with it, safe-cracking might seem like an easier way to pass the time. The good news is, squash is an incredibly versatile and forgiving old devil, and will stand up to cooking inaccuracies far more favourably than more fragile specimens. And when cooked until soft then blitzed to a purée, as in this butternut squash cheesecake (recipe overleaf), it's as velvety textured and gloriously tasty as any vegetable you'll encounter. And let's not forget the seeds that so frivolously get consigned to the bin: toast them in the oven, sprinkle them with sea salt and enjoy a healthy snack for almost free!

Whole roasted squash

Uses: 1 whole butternut squash, olive oil, seasoning

Peeling a whole squash can be a pain and can easily demolish a sub-standard peeler, so don't bother unless you really have to. It's hard to imagine that such a thick skin will become beautifully soft after just under 1 hour in the oven, but it does – and looks good too. To achieve this minor feat of culinary alchemy, preheat the oven to 180°C (Gas Mark 4). Cut the squash lengthways through the middle and drizzle with a little olive oil and seasoning. Place the halves flesh side down on a baking tray and roast for 45 minutes.

Butternut squash cheesecake

This cheesecake tastes great and looks impressive too. The chilli-and-cheese-breadcrumb base is a marvellous savoury twist on the traditional sweet biscuit base.

Serves 6

For the savoury crumb base:
130g butter, plus extra for greasing
210g chilli and cheese breadcrumbs
(page 54)

For the filling:
1 medium to large butternut squash
1 tbsp olive oil, plus extra for drizzling
1 tsp fresh thyme
seasoning
small knob of butter
2 tbsp cornflour
500g cream cheese
2 eggs
2 tbsp crème fraîche
200g feta, crumbled

You will also need: spring-form cake tin (23cm diameter) or similar

Preheat the oven to 200°C (Gas Mark 6). Line a spring-form cake tin with baking parchment and grease it lightly with butter. Melt 130g butter and stir it into the chilli and cheese breadcrumbs. Tip the mix into the lined tin and spread evenly while pressing down firmly.

For the filling, peel the squash and cut off the bulbous end. Slice it in half and scoop out the seeds, separating them from the fibrous strands. Bake the seeds for about 10 minutes and set aside.

Slice the bulbous end of the squash as thinly as possible and cut the remaining squash into approximately 2cm cubes. Spread them on a baking tray, drizzle with a little olive oil, sprinkle over the thyme and season. Bake in the hot oven for 10-15 minutes, or until they start to brown and are cooked through. Set aside and cool.

Meanwhile, make the squash purée. Put the 1 tbsp oil and butter in a heavy-based pan with a lid over a medium heat. When hot, add the squash slices, cover and cook on a low to medium heat for about 10 minutes, or until soft. Set aside to cool.

Lower the oven temperature to 180°C (Gas Mark 4). Put the cornflour and cream cheese into a large bowl and whisk together (cornflour first so it doesn't fly everywhere!). Next, beat in the eggs, then the crème fraîche. Stir in the crumbled feta then (gently) the squash purée. For an attractive orange marbled effect, just don't mix it in fully.

Pour the mixture into the prepared cake tin and spread evenly across the top. Cover loosely with foil, and place in the centre of the oven. Bake for 30 minutes then remove the foil. Bake for a further 20 minutes, or until the top feels set to the touch. Remove from the oven and allow to cool for about 2 hours.

Once cooled, remove the cake tin surround. Arrange the roasted cubes on top of the cheesecake and sprinkle over the toasted squash seeds. Store covered in the fridge.

Butternut squash and goats' cheese risotto

This is a brilliant dinner-party dish, as risotto lends itself well to the par-cooking process (see page 25), and the squash additions can be prepared days in advance.

Serves 4

For the squash purée:
1 large butternut squash
seasoning
75g unsalted butter

For the risotto base:
1.5 litres chicken or vegetable stock
2 tbsp oil
1 onion, finely chopped
2 garlic cloves, crushed
1 dsp chopped fresh thyme
400g risotto rice
250ml white wine (optional)

To serve:
250g goats' cheese
75g Parmesan, freshly grated

You will also need: stick blender or food processor

Preheat the oven to 180°C (Gas Mark 4). Peel and cut off the end of the squash, slice it in half and scrape out and bake the seeds, as in the cheesecake recipe (see opposite). Cut the bulbous end into thin slices and the remainder of the squash into approximately 1cm cubes.

Increase the oven temperature to 200°C (Gas Mark 6). Spread the cubes on a baking tray. Season, drizzle with olive oil and roast until just tender, about 15-20 minutes.

To make the squash purée, melt the butter in a heavy-based pan and add the squash slices. Gently cook until very soft, about 20 minutes. Add a little water if necessary. When cooked, blend to a purée with a stick blender or food processor. Season and set aside to cool.

To make the risotto, pour the stock into a pan and bring to a low simmer. In another heavy-based pan, heat 2 tbsp oil and gently cook the onion, garlic and thyme until soft. Add the rice and stir for 2 minutes. Add the wine (if using) and stir constantly until absorbed. Then and 2 ladles of stock and stir until most of the liquid has been absorbed. Repeat this process until the rice is cooked al dente, about 15-20 minutes.

About 2-3 minutes before serving, stir in the squash purée and crumble in the goats' cheese. Re-heat the squash cubes and add most of the Parmesan to the risotto. To serve, garnish with the squash cubes, the rest of the Parmesan and the lightly toasted seeds.

For other recipe ideas for butternut squash, see:

Vegetable tagine (page 65)
Leftover roast chicken dinner stuffed squash (page 141)

Cabbage

Cabbage I always use savoy rather than white cabbage simply because I prefer the flavour, and I can also use the larger, thicker outer leaves, which normally get discarded, as an edible wrap for leftovers.

Simple shredded cabbage

Uses: butter, cabbage, seasoning

As well as being quick, simple and tasty, this dish can be re-heated with a whole stack of cooked leftovers, such as chopped sausage and bacon, poached or roast chicken, a spoonful of cream cheese or grated Cheddar. Heat a mug of water and a tablespoon of butter in a large heavy-based frying pan. Add 2 handfuls of shredded cabbage and good dose of seasoning. Cook for 2-3 minutes, remove from the heat and drain off any excess liquid. If you're not using the cabbage straight away, spread it out in a thin layer to allow it to cool down quickly and evenly before refrigerating in an airtight container.

Stuffed cabbage leaves

Uses: cabbage leaves with optional fillings (see box opposite)

Cabbage leaf parcels make a marvellous main dish in their own right. They are fabulous filled with rice and couscous, then gently steamed for maximum flavour and goodness. Placed on a little pool of vibrant roast red pepper and tomato sauce (page 64), they make a colourful addition to a dinner-party table.

Four fillings for stuffed cabbage leaves

★ *Shredded creamed cabbage with Cheddar and pancetta (see opposite)*
★ *Kedgeree mix (page 116) – just wrap the mix in the leaves instead of coating in the flour, egg and breadcrumbs as you would for the fishcakes*
★ *Top-tasting couscous (see page 125)*
★ *Chicken and pea biryani (see page146)*

> **🍲 To blanch outer cabbage leaves** Using a sharp pointed knife, carefully score the cabbage around the root to release the thick outer leaves. Boil a large pan of slightly salted water and dunk in the leaves, pressing them down to submerge them completely. Boil for 1 minute, then remove and put into a bowl of the coldest water possible (iced, ideally). Then run the cold tap over the leaves for 2 minutes to stop the cooking process. Drain them well and lay out on kitchen paper to dry thoroughly. They're now ready to fill with whatever you fancy. Just put the mixture in the middle, wrap the leaves around and then turn over, tucking the leaf edges underneath to form a closed parcel.

Shredded creamed cabbage with Cheddar and pancetta

Any leftover meat would be an excellent addition to this creamy mix. Or, use shredded cabbage that has already been cooked and refrigerated – add to the hot, reduced cream mix to warm through.

Serves 2 as a side dish

oil for frying
handful of pancetta or bacon bits
half a cabbage, finely sliced
150ml double cream
handful of grated Cheddar
seasoning

Place a heavy-based frying pan over a medium–high heat, add a little oil and, when very hot, add the pancetta or bacon bits. Fry for 2 minutes, until they start to go brown, then add the cabbage, cream and cheese. Reduce the heat and simmer for a few minutes until the cream has thickened and has coated and cooked the cabbage.

Season to taste and either serve immediately or cool and refrigerate for later.

For other recipe ideas for cabbage, see:

Pancakes: four gourmet pancake fillings (shredded creamed cabbage, etc.) (page 36)
Perfect omelette: five omelette fillings (shredded creamed cabbage, etc.) (page 42)

Carrots

My carrots generally appear in a plastic bag. So, first things first: lose the bag as quickly as possible and substitute it with bubble wrap, then a dampened J cloth. This method of storage protects and allows air circulation at the same time. You can now stash them in the fridge. Carrots can be frozen prior to being used in a recipe if you blanch them first. Just drop them into boiling water for a few minutes, refresh under cold running water then freeze in a ziplock plastic bag.

What happens, then, when in spite of all preventative measures, we still wind up with wrinkly, bendy, black-blotched offerings? Scratch beneath the surface! They may be bendy, they may be covered in black blotches, they may even need a few green patches cutting away, but after a good peel and a refreshing dip into ice-cold water, chances are they're ready for anything – especially when grated and mixed up with other ingredients. Remember also that carrots are what cumin was invented for: bland and boring carrots become flavoursome and exotic when enhanced by a few North African spices.

Carrot, onion and cumin fritters

This recipe was inspired by Nigel Slater, the grand master of full-flavoured every-day cooking. It's a masterclass in creating a mouth-watering dish from the most basic ingredients, in no time at all for practically nothing. You can also fry these little morsels in batches then simply re-heat them on a baking tray in the oven when you need them.

Makes about 9 two-bite fritters

1 carrot, grated
1 onion, finely sliced
2 tbsp flour

3 tbsp double cream, or crème fraîche
1 tsp ground cumin
seasoning
oil for frying

Combine all the ingredients, except the oil, in a bowl.

Heat a heavy-based, non-stick frying pan on a medium–high heat and add the oil. Scoop up a tablespoon of mixture and form into a more solid mass with your other hand while still on the spoon. Gently lower the tablespoon of mixture into the frying pan, pressing down gently with the back of the spoon. Repeat the process until you've used all the mixture.

Fry each fritter for 3-4 minutes on each side, or until deep golden brown. Remove them from the pan and drain on kitchen paper to remove excess oil.

Cauliflower

Plain boiled cauliflower is about as uninspiring as vegetables can get. But start adding complementary ingredients such as bacon, cheese, smoked fish and white sauce and it's a whole different story. And don't fear the cauli blotch either – that outer floret discolouration is no reason to ditch it.

Luxury cauliflower mash

This is very much a naughty-but-nice luxury purée. If you happen to have a little bottle of white truffle oil stashed at the very back of your scary cupboard, now is the time for it to take centre stage. Go easy though – it packs a powerful punch.

Serves 4

45g butter
1 cauliflower, sliced
170ml double cream
splash of milk
550g potatoes, peeled and cut into large, even-sized chunks
seasoning

You will also need: potato ricer; stick blender

Heat the butter in a pan over a medium heat. Add the cauliflower in a single layer and cook for 3-4 minutes until just starting to colour, then turn the slices over. Add the cream and just a splash of milk (the liquid should come about halfway up the slices). Cook on a low heat (gently bubbling) for about 15 minutes, or until tender.

Put the potatoes into a pan of cold salted water. Bring to the boil and then simmer until the potatoes are cooked through. Drain well and mash, ideally using a potato ricer.

Blend the cooked cauliflower mixture to a smooth purée using a stick blender and fold into the mashed potato. Adjust the seasoning to taste.

Top mash variations

★ Caramelised onion and sage mash: slowly fold in caramelised onions and finely chopped sage.
★ Celeriac mash: peel and chop the celeriac, barely cover with double cream and cook on a low heat till soft. Season, purée, then fold into the mash.
★ Roast garlic (page 83) mash: squeeze the garlic into the mash to taste.

Smoked haddock cauliflower cheese on chargrilled baguette

Cauliflower cheese is another of those abiding childhood memories that fills us with comfort. I've spruced it up a bit here. Of course this 'cauliflower plus other ingredient' combo would also work beautifully with bacon or sliced cooked sausage. Or put the cauliflower on a layer of sliced cooked potato before popping it in the oven.

Serves 4 as a side tapas-style dish

50g butter, plus extra for greasing
1 cauliflower, broken into florets
200g smoked haddock
450ml milk
fresh parsley stalks
1 bay leaf
50g plain flour
seasoning
100g Cheddar, grated

Preheat the oven to 200°C (Gas Mark 6).

Lightly butter an ovenproof dish that will hold the cauliflower florets snugly. Cook the cauliflower florets in a pan of slightly salted boiling water for 3 minutes. Drain well and tip them into the prepared dish.

Put the smoked haddock in a pan, pour in the milk and add the parsley stalks and bay leaf. Bring to a simmer then remove from the heat and leave to stand for 5 minutes. Remove the smoked haddock and set aside.

Melt the butter in a pan over a low heat, add the flour and cook for 2 minutes, stirring continuously.

Strain the hot milk through a sieve then gradually pour it over the flour and butter roux over a low heat, whisking continuously to create a smooth sauce. Add the grated cheese, leaving a little aside, and stir until smooth and melted. Season to taste with salt and pepper.

Flake the smoked haddock and tuck it in among the florets. Pour over the sauce, top with the rest of the grated cheese and bake in the oven for 15 minutes.

For other recipe ideas for cauliflower, see:

Vegetable tagine (page 65)

Courgettes

They may have gone a little bendy and lost that new-look lustre, but that's no reason for binning them. My favourite and, I reckon, the tastiest way to cook courgettes is by chargrilling long strips. They also offer great versatility. Once cooled they can be stored in an airtight container in the fridge for days and then quickly chopped and thrown into a pasta sauce, lasagne mix or pie-and-pastry filling. Alternatively, whole strips can be heated in the oven as a vegetable side dish, while finely diced into pieces they make an excellent addition to that ever-evolving couscous, rice or pasta salad.

Chargrilled courgette strips

Uses: courgettes, olive oil, seasoning

Put a griddle pan over a high heat to preheat for at least 10 minutes. Slice the courgettes into 2-5mm strips. If you want to use them as whole slices, keep them thin, but if you're planning to chop them, keep them thicker. Lay them out on a tray and douse liberally with olive oil and seasoning. Transfer to the hot griddle pan and leave for 1-2 minutes, until nicely marked with the griddle bars. Turn over and cook the other side. Remove from the pan and lay out in a single layer to cool down.

For other recipe ideas for courgettes, see:

Change your thinking: salsatastic! (mango and courgette) (page 16)
Whatever-you-want flan (page 40)
Vegetable tagine (page 65)
Spanish tortilla (page 92)
Potato *Rösti* (page 93)
Composite salads: ideas for composite salads (courgettes – chargrilled and sliced (page 131)
Sausage, courgettes and peas in tomato sauce (page 145)

Fennel
I love fennel. Thinly sliced in its raw state, it adds pizzazz to an otherwise dull salad. It makes a superb complement to chicken and fish, and roughly chopped gives a depth of flavour to a medley of the most ordinary roasted veg (see Whole baked bream on roasted veg, page 115). Pan-fried in butter then braised in a little stock, fennel becomes meltingly tender. And whatever you do, don't bin those fabulous dill-like fronds. They're free herbs!

Honey and lemon braised fennel

This is one of my all-time favourite veggie side dishes. It's so good that I serve it tapas-style in its own right – glazed under the grill in its own little dish. The fennel becomes beautifully soft, while the combination of sharp citrus, sweet honey and aniseed tick just about every flavour box in the book. Remove the zest from the lemons before you squeeze them so you can save it or just mix it in with the stock.

Serves 4 as a veggie side dish, or individual tapas

4 fennel bulbs
160g butter
400ml chicken stock
juice of 4 lemons
4 tsp runny honey
40g Parmesan, freshly grated

Preheat the oven to 180°C (Gas Mark 4).

To prepare the fennel bulbs, cut off the leafy fronds and reserve them for garnish or later use. Slice each bulb in half then cut each half into 3 wedges – or 4 if the fennel is particularly large.

Gently heat the butter in a pan large enough to accommodate all the fennel wedges in a single layer. If necessary, cook the fennel in two pans. Place the fennel wedges, flat side down, in the pan and cook gently until they start to brown. Turn and repeat on the other flat side, then finally brown their rounded side.

Pour over the stock, lemon juice and honey. Cook very gently for about 20 minutes, or until the fennel is just tender. Remove and set aside.

Strain the cooking liquor through a fine sieve, return to the pan and cook until reduced by half – the sauce should be quite thick. Remove from the heat.

Place the fennel in an ovenproof dish, pour over the sauce and then sprinkle with grated Parmesan. Bake in the preheated oven for 15 minutes. Remove and serve garnished with the fennel fronds.

Garlic

Garlic Bulbs with green sprouting roots are invariably the biggest reason for binning garlic. As it happens, these young green shoots are bitter and can cause indigestion, so you're probably right to consign them to the compost. However, the secret to keeping garlic is to roast the whole bulb before it ever gets to this point, turning its flesh into a smooth and unctuous purée – a far cry from its less sophisticated raw or pan-fried alter ego. Remarkably it's just about the easiest culinary transformation you will ever undertake – and, believe me, this little trick will change your culinary landscape for ever.

Roast garlic

Uses: whole garlic bulbs

To perform this piece of culinary magic, preheat the oven to 180°C (Gas Mark 4). Then simply wrap the whole bulbs loosely in foil and roast in the oven for 1-1½ hours, depending on the size of the bulbs. When ready, they should be soft and squidgy when squeezed. If you're not sure, open one up, cut in half around the middle, and you should squeeze out a gorgeous light tan purée. If it's not quite ready, rewrap and put back in the oven for a little longer. You can rewrap the roasted half or whole bulbs in foil and freeze them until required. Try roast garlic in mashed potato (awesome), in flatbread with cooked sausage (page 55), combined with cheesy mushrooms (page 85), squeezed over hot roasted veg, or spread thinly over bruschetta with chopped tomato, olive oil and herbs. It also adds a deep, rich garlic flavour to many recipes.

Think roast Roast garlic can be used in any dish that includes garlic! You should see it as a valuable addition to your armoury of flavourings and seasonings.

Mushrooms

Two key things to remember here about storage: not in or under plastic, and not in the fridge. A cool, dark, dry place is best, or just in a brown paper bag in the veg rack. Once cooked, cooled, covered and refrigerated, they will hold their flavour and texture without going dry, blotchy or wrinkled. If

mushrooms do go past their prime, they will still give a top flavour if swiftly cooked with good seasoning, and the cooking process will eliminate any chewiness. They can be re-heated in pretty much any way you fancy, e.g. whole in the oven or in a pan with a sauce. They also make a tasty little composite salad contribution (page 131).

Baked flat-cap mushrooms

Uses: flat-cap mushrooms, butter and/or olive oil, seasoning, fresh thyme or oregano, garlic (the herbs and garlic are optional)

Baking is one of my favourite ways to cook flat-cap mushrooms, as it retains maximum juiciness, gives even cooking and infuses them with herby seasoning. Preheat the oven to 180°C (Gas Mark 4). Arrange the mushrooms, gill side up, in a single layer in an ovenproof dish. Dot with butter or drizzle with olive oil (or both) and season well with salt and pepper. You can add a few sprigs of fresh thyme or oregano and slivers of garlic for extra flavour. Cover with foil and bake in the oven for about 20 minutes, or until tender. Add them to the roast and chargrilled vegetable tart (page 64), spread them on toast topped with scrambled egg for breakfast, or slice them up and mix them into your favourite pasta dish.

Creamed mustard mushrooms

Uses: mushrooms, oil and butter, cream, wholegrain or Dijon mustard, chopped parsley, seasoning

Just fry the mushrooms in a little oil and butter over a high heat for 2 minutes then add a good slug of cream. Boil the cream for a few more seconds to reduce it to a thick coating then add 1 tsp mustard and a handful of chopped parsley and job done! A final dose of seasoning and you've got a tasty topping for toast, baked potato or *Rösti* in less than five minutes – and another veg-rack remnant saved from a miserable demise.

Cheesy roast garlic mushrooms

Spoon on to toast or use as a filling for jacket potatoes (page 87), pancakes and Yorkshire puddings.

Makes enough to fill 2 giant jacket-potato halves, or about 8 mini Yorkshire puds

15g butter
175g mushrooms, sliced
2 tbsp cream cheese
100g Cheddar, grated
2 spring onions, finely chopped
half a roast garlic bulb (page 83)

To garnish:
1 tbsp chopped fresh parsley

Melt the butter in a frying pan and cook the mushrooms until tender. Stir in the cream cheese, grated Cheddar and spring onions, squeeze in the roast garlic and stir until melted and combined.

Remove from the heat and garnish with chopped fresh parsley.

For other recipe ideas for mushrooms, see:

Yorkshire puddings: five gourmet Yorkshire pudding fillings (cheesy roast garlic mushrooms) (page 35)
Pancakes: four tempting pancake fillings (cheesy roast garlic mushrooms) (page 36)
Stuffed jacket potato: four luxury fillings for jacket potato (cheesy roast garlic mushrooms) (page 87)
Composite salads: ideas for composite salads (button mushrooms – sliced and sautéd (page 131)

Potatoes

There's something about the humble tattie that warms the culinary soul like no other vegetable. A ubiquitous part of our eating landscape, the potato is never more than a fork's reach away. From fast-food dinner to haute cuisine; from baked, boiled and roasted to croquettes, potato pancakes, tortillas and even bread. Perhaps it's this unrivalled versatility that so endears us. The only problem a potato glut should cause is choosing a recipe from the vast repertoire available.

Before we start, a quick word on storage. While potatoes seem to last for ever in the fridge, the starch will turn to sugar, which can spoil flavour. New potatoes are low in starch and therefore more suited to fridge storage. However, their shelf life is much shorter than that of their floury cousins. Old, larger, floury potatoes can last up to six months if kept in a cool, dark, dry place with plenty of ventilation. Whatever you do, make sure you take them out of plastic bags as soon as possible and transfer them to a paper bag or wrap them in newspaper. Plastic bags cause sweating and dampness, resulting in rotting. If potatoes have a green hue to their skin, avoid. This is caused by sunlight, which creates a toxic chemical called solanine, so it means the end of your poor tattie.

Stuffed jacket potato

Uses: floury potato, olive oil, seasoning, filling of your choice

If you think the modest jacket is just a side veg for a mid-week dinner, then think again. Thick-skinned or not, with just a few additions from the fridge, store cupboard or veg rack, this floury fella can become a full-on dinner in its own right. The potato can be baked in advance because the whole package can be assembled cold then re-heated without any loss in quality.

Preheat the oven to 200°C (Gas Mark 6). Wash and dry the potato, prick with a fork then rub with a little olive oil and scatter with sea salt. Bake for about 1½ hours until golden brown and crisp on the outside. To speed things up and save energy, give the potato a blast in the microwave for about 10 minutes (prick the skin first) and then transfer it to the oven to get that scrumptious roasted skin.

Once baked, allow the potato to cool, cut it in half and then scoop out the fluffy flesh into a bowl big enough to accommodate your filling (see below). Either combine the filling with the potato flesh, season to taste, then spoon the mixture back into the potato skin. Or use the jacket as a vessel for the other ingredients then top with the mashed potato – a bit like a cottage, shepherd's or fish pie.

Four luxury fillings for jacket potato

★ Baked beans and red onion
★ Cottage cheese, chives and tinned tuna, topped with grated Cheddar
★ Fish pie jacket: try tinned salmon, prawns, double cream and spring onions
★ Cheesy roast garlic mushrooms (page 85)

Roast new potato brunch

This is just the treat to set you up for lazy Sundays on the sofa, eating, reading and watching TV. Roast potatoes with fried egg topping is a superb way to use up new potatoes that won't quite cut the mustard when boiled until tender and served with a little mint and butter. Everything else is optional, and can be chopped and changed according to mood and what you have on hand. Try finely sliced red pepper (cooked or otherwise), sautéd mushrooms, sliced cooked onions or especially leftover chilli. Chorizo, by the way, is awesome. Just throw it in with the potatoes about 5 minutes before they've finished roasting.

Serves 2

1 bay leaf (dry or fresh)
1 tsp dried rosemary, or similar seasoning
2 tbsp oil, plus extra for frying
2 handfuls (about 300g) of new potatoes
2-4 slices cooked bacon, cut into small pieces
200g cooked black pudding, chopped or crumbled

handful or 2 of robust salad leaves, such as a spinach, rocket or watercress combo
2 eggs
chopped fresh parsley

You will also need: stick blender with bowl attachment

Preheat the oven to 200°C (Gas Mark 6).

Blitz the bay leaf, rosemary, seasoning and oil with a stick blender with bowl attachment.

Coat the potatoes in the herb oil and spread on a roasting tray in a single layer. Roast in the preheated oven for about 30 minutes, or until golden and cooked through.

Remove from the oven and mix with the bacon, black pudding and salad leaves. Keep the mixture warm while you fry the eggs.

Put the potato mix into a serving plate or bowl and top with the fried egg and chopped parsley.

Cheesy potato garlic dip

I guarantee this dip will turn a few eye-ridden tatties into a truly sumptuous dip to warm the soul on the dreariest of winter nights. When you add the cheese and olive oil, remember that kitchen mantra of non-recipe cooking: *you can add but you can't take away.* Just taste as you go along and decide when you've got a texture and flavour to die for.

4 medium-sized (about 400g) all-rounder potatoes (e.g. Maris Piper), peeled and any eyes removed
2 eggs, boiled for 8 minutes
a generous lump of cheese (I used about 90g medium Cheddar), grated
half a roast garlic bulb (page 83)
100ml olive oil
seasoning to taste
crostini (page 54) or flatbread (page 55) for dipping

You will also need: potato ricer

Put the potatoes in a pan and cover with cold, salted water. Bring to the boil and simmer until cooked through.

Meanwhile, press the boiled eggs through a fine sieve with the back of a ladle or spoon.

Drain the cooked potatoes, getting rid of any surplus moisture, and mash using a potato ricer. While still warm, beat in the eggs and cheese and squeeze in the roast garlic. Then beat in a little oil at a time until you've got a smooth dip.

Season to taste and serve with a stack of crostini (page 54) or home-made flatbread (page 55). Alternatively, see the case study below for inspiration.

CASE STUDY

A veg-rack salvation

After making this wonderfully tasty cheesy potato garlic dip, I popped it into the freezer. Fast-forward a few weeks and after a check of the veg rack – a bundle of gifted allotment-grown carrots and a pack of asparagus – and I dig it out to defrost. A quick boil of the veg, immediately refreshed under cold water to stop the cooking process and cool down, and I've got the perfect dipping condiments for a delicious free dinner with Monday-night footie. No stress, just a few minutes of cooking and I ain't spent a penny.

Warm potato salad

If your idea of a potato salad is a few cubes of bland potato drowning in gloopy mayonnaise, it's time to reconsider. That bag of new potatoes is your route to creating tasty dishes for next to nothing. Result! I've made potato salads – or écrasé potatoes in fancy restaurant-speak – hundreds of times and rarely have I made them exactly the same twice. There's always something you've got lying around – perhaps lemon zest, chilli oil, diced tomato, fennel fronds or celery leaves – that will give them a unique twist and transform the ordinary to the sublime.

Serves 3-4 as a side dish

2-3 handfuls (about 500g) of new potatoes
1 tbsp chopped shallots
1 tbsp chopped spring onion
2 tbsp parsley oil (page 99)
1 tbsp plain yoghurt
1 tsp chopped capers
seasoning

Put the potatoes in a pan of slightly salted boiling water and simmer until just tender. Drain well then return to the heat for a few seconds to get rid of any residual moisture.

Transfer the potatoes to a mixing bowl and, while still warm, add the shallots. Lightly crush the potatoes with the ends of a fork.

Add the remaining ingredients and salt and pepper to taste. Serve warm, at room temperature or from the fridge.

Potato pancakes

Otherwise known as crêpes parmentier, these little fellas will impress dinner guests with a bit of tempting finger food, and they're infinitely tastier than shop-bought blinis, which to me taste of cardboard. Topped with a little flaked poached or smoked salmon and a smidgen of sour cream or crème fraîche, they're perfect party food. Alternatively, make one big blini as a base for a pile of scrambled egg and crispy bacon for an indulgent Sunday brunch.

Makes 7 bite-sized blinis

150g potatoes (Maris Piper, King Edward or similar), peeled and cut into even-sized chunks
1 dsp double cream
1 dsp milk
1 dsp plain flour
1 egg
1 egg white (save the yolk for hollandaise sauce – see page 45)
oil for frying

You will also need: potato ricer; whisk

Place the potatoes in a pan and cover with cold salted water. Bring to the boil then simmer until fully cooked through. Drain well, return to the pan and heat for a few seconds to steam off excess moisture.

Mash the potatoes by passing through a potato ricer and allow to cool.

Blend the mashed potatoes and other pancake ingredients using a whisk, then press the mixture through a fine sieve using the back of a ladle or a large spoon.

To make the pancakes, heat a non-stick frying pan and very lightly grease the base of it with an oiled piece of kitchen paper (be careful!). Spoon 1 tbsp of mixture into the pan, cook until lightly browned then gently flip it over and cook on the other side. Slide on to a plate, cover to keep warm and repeat the process with the remaining batter.

Spanish tortilla

This is a classic example of how the Spanish are second to none at taking two or three basic ingredients and transforming them into flavour heaven. I don't care how tired and old those potatoes and onions look (as long as they're still edible and the potatoes aren't green) – gentle, careful cooking and good seasoning will coax out every last bit of flavour. Just don't compromise on the eggs – ever! While a traditional tortilla requires nothing more than potato, onion, eggs and seasoning, it can form the base for all manner of everyday ingredients and leftovers. The one in the photo includes chopped chargrilled courgette strips, which I had in the fridge. I was spoilt for choice as to what to use them for, but the tortilla plan swung it. Other past additions have included roasted red pepper, chopped cooked sausage and bacon, and even tinned fish.

Serves 3-4

4 tbsp oil
2-3 large potatoes (about 500g), thinly sliced
1 large onion, thinly sliced
6 eggs, beaten
chargrilled courgette strips (page 81), sliced
seasoning

*You will **also need:*** (ideally) small heavy-based frying pan, about 24cm diameter and 4cm deep

Heat 3 tbsp oil in a heavy-based frying pan and gently cook the potatoes and onion until soft, about 20 minutes. Stir regularly to avoid the potatoes sticking. Drain off the oil and set aside.

Beat the eggs in a large bowl then add the courgette strips, cooked potatoes and onion. Mix thoroughly and season well.

Heat the remaining 1 tbsp oil in the frying pan, pour in the tortilla mixture and cook over a low heat for 8-10 minutes. Towards the end of cooking, preheat the grill to medium then finish the tortilla under the grill until golden brown on top and just set.

Leave to stand then turn out on to a flat plate and serve warm or cold.

My tortilla heaven

A common battle cry of traditional waste-haters is "Just buy what you need". But, while admirable, this can't always be practised (buy one, get one free – what are you going to do?). The principle extends to "Just cook what you need", but again this doesn't always work. After finding myself with a glut of potatoes and onions, and really wanting to make only one tortilla for immediate eating, it made sense to cook all the potatoes and onions rather than let them deteriorate in the veg rack. I then had a ready-made tortilla base that simply needed the addition of eggs at a later date – definitely the quickest bit of tortilla cooking and economical too.

Potato *Rösti*

Uses: good-sized floury potatoes, seasoning, other (optional) ingredients of your choice, oil for frying

I could fill an entire book with *Rösti* recipes alone, but you don't need that when you can create your own magical repertoire from the basic dish – a pile of par-cooked, grated potato and seasoning. The amount of potato depends on how big a *Rösti* you want, and a variety of ingredients can be added: thinly sliced onion, chilli flakes,

finely chopped fresh chillies, cooked bacon, grated carrot, grated cheese, grated courgette, fresh herbs, dried herbs. To prepare the potatoes, peel and cut into quarters then put into salted cold water. Bring to the boil and simmer for about 5 minutes. Drain well, allow to cool, then grate. Add a generous amount of salt and pepper, and any other ingredients, then shape into patties. Fry in a little oil over a medium heat until golden brown.

For other recipe ideas for potatoes, see:

Composite salads: ideas for composite salads (new potatoes – roast and halved or sliced and boiled) (page 131)

Red peppers

OK, own up – who's thrown away peppers just because they've gone a bit wrinkly? They may not have the same crunch when eaten raw in a salad or as part of a crudité selection, but roasting them or chucking them in a stir-fry will soon bring them back to their full-flavoured former selves.

I've selected red peppers here simply because they are the only type I seem to use, with the exception of the occasional green pepper in a stir-fry. They just seem to have more flavour, look tastier and roast better. But I'm sure you've got your own preferences, so just adapt the recipes accordingly.

Roasted whole red peppers

Uses: whole peppers!

This process couldn't be easier. Preheat the oven to 180°C (Gas Mark 4), stick the whole pepper in an ovenproof dish and roast for 30-40 minutes, or until the skin starts to blister all over. Remove and transfer to another container then immediately wrap in cling film and leave to cool. When unwrapped you'll find the papery skin just peels off to leave you with a bright red, tender, tasty pepper – and loads of juice to enhance any tomato-based sauce or soup. The pepper can be cut into thin strips for a vibrant garnish, thrown into a composite salad or blitzed into a delicious purée for adding to anything from pasta to pesto.

Stuffed red pepper tuna melts

A classic example of how everyday random ingredients can be transformed into dinner-party heaven. Again, this recipe is just a guideline. Any number of ingredients can be added to the melting white sauce filling – cooked chicken, tinned or cooked fresh fish, chopped-up cooked veg, a few spoonfuls of leftover Bolognese sauce . . . The list is only restricted by what you have and your imagination. And what you serve it with is equally unrestricted – I served this particular version with blanched asparagus and parsley oil (see page 99).

Serves 2

2 roasted red peppers (page 94)
half a serving of white sauce (page 44)
1 tin tuna, drained well
about 30g cheese (depending on type and strength – just taste as you go)

Preheat the oven to 180°C (Gas Mark 4).

Carefully remove the stalks and skins from the peppers, being careful not to tear the flesh.

If your white sauce is cold, heat it gently in a saucepan then add the tuna and cheese. Keep stirring until the cheese has melted.

Carefully spoon the mixture into the peppers and close them up into a parcel. To serve, warm through in the preheated oven for 10-15 minutes.

For other recipe ideas for peppers, see:

Egg, anchovy and roast pepper bruschetta (page 39)
Composite salads: ideas for composite salads (roasted red pepper – peeled and sliced in strips) (page 131)

Tomatoes

Tomatoes Of all the supermarket fruit and veg, tomatoes in particular are cultivated for shelf life at the expense of flavour. Rather ironically, I reckon this is why we end up binning them – because they simply don't taste of anything worthwhile. The classic waste scenario involves squidgy tomatoes that have magically started to split their skins. It's at this point that most people mistakenly believe they are finished and consign them to the bin. In actual fact, for those thick-skinned, long-life supermarket varieties, this is when they're at optimum flavour. And although they may not look too appetising as a sandwich ingredient, they're in prime shape for a rich sauce or soup. Ideally, uncooked tomatoes should not be stored in the fridge, as this will kill off whatever lingering flavour there may be. As with most fruit and veg, a cool, dark, dry place is the ideal option.

Oven-roasted tomatoes

Uses: tomatoes, olive oil, dried or fresh herbs, seasoning

When you're faced with a sudden glut of tomatoes decaying in front of your very eyes, roast them! Preheat the oven to 150°C (Gas Mark 2), cut the offending toms in half, then place them in a single layer on a baking tray lined with baking parchment. Drizzle with olive oil, add seasoning and herbs, then roast in the oven for 1½ hours. You can chop them up for salads, blitz them in a blender with stock for a roast tomato sauce or soup, or add chunks to your favourite pasta dish. They will last for a good couple of weeks in an airtight container in the fridge, and indefinitely if you cover them in a layer of oil – giving you the added bonus of a lovely tomato-infused oil. Alternatively, layer them between layers of baking parchment and freeze.

Rich tomato passata

Making your own rich passata-style sauce is easier and quicker than you might think. It's also going to be infinitely tastier than the shop-bought jars. Passata is incredibly versatile and freezes without a problem, so you'll be able to knock up a tasty tea in minutes. Passata is also a base sauce for any number of cooked leftovers: think pasta, pizza or the roast and chargrilled vegetable tart on page 64.

The essential constituents of this sauce are slowly caramelised onions, herbs and any kind of tomato – fresh, tinned or a combination of the two – but adapt as you wish. Use dried or fresh herbs, such as Italian mixed herbs or fresh oregano, but any coarse herbs will give fabulous flavour. The secret here is to slowly simmer away the water content to concentrate the flavours and achieve a rich, dark red, paste-like sauce. You can always add a bit of stock or water later for a looser consistency.

Makes enough for a main course pasta dish for 2

oil for frying
1 onion, thinly sliced
1 dsp tomato purée
2 tomatoes, roughly chopped
1 tin chopped tomatoes
1 dsp dried mixed herbs
2 garlic cloves, crushed (or purée from half a roast garlic bulb – page 83)

Heat the oil in a frying pan and fry the onions on a gentle heat for about 15 minutes, until caramelised. Add the tomato purée and cook for 2 minutes then add all the other ingredients.

Slowly simmer for about 15 minutes, until the desired consistency is reached – the longer the sauce cooks, the darker the colour and richer the flavour.

For other recipe ideas for tomatoes, see:

Roast and chargrilled vegetable tart with roast red pepper and tomato sauce (page 64)
Instant tortilla pizza (page 143)
Sausage, courgettes and peas in tomato sauce (page 145)

Fresh herbs

Fresh herbs A good selection of fresh herbs is one of the most enjoyable and simplest ways to transform the mundane into the gourmet. Yet, sadly, supermarket packets of fresh herbs seem to deteriorate instantly once opened. The best solution is to grow your own. But if you don't have the time, patience or inclination, the secret of extra-long herb life is to follow the simple steps below – infinitely preferable to buying those little pots of herbs. Along with my roasted garlic, this top tip features in just about every cooking demo I give, simply because of the feedback I get from people who use it. It's nothing short of magic!

Storing fresh herbs This storage method applies only to fragile herbs: chervil, chives, coriander, dill, parsley and tarragon (but not basil). Coarse herbs, such as thyme and rosemary, can of course be used dry. This method can also revitalise wilted herbs. I have kept flat leaf parsley for up to three weeks using this method, with just slightly yellowing outer leaves in week three.

1. Remove the herbs from the packet when first bought and bin the bag.

2. Take a piece or two of kitchen paper, or an unused J cloth, and roll up the herbs in the paper or cloth.

3. Sprinkle cold water all over the paper or cloth to lightly dampen – not saturate.

4. Finally, wrap in cling film and store in the fridge.

5. Each time you use the herbs, just re-roll the rest in the same wrapping. Replace the paper or cloth if it starts to discolour.

Herb oils

Making vibrant green oils out of your herbs gives you an instant, no-heating-required sauce to drizzle around any number of dishes, from fishcakes to poached chicken salad, tarts, omelettes and Spanish tortilla. Remember that olive oil is a preservative, so this way you're giving fragile herbs weeks of tasty shelf life.

Sauce vierge

This is based on another of those recipes that pops up in top establishments, yet uses basic ingredients that can be prepared in less than five minutes. The classic recipe uses basil, but feel free to use any combination of fragile herbs: basil, chervil, chives, coriander, dill and parsley will all work well here.

75ml extra virgin olive oil
2 tomatoes, skinned, deseeded and chopped into small dice
1 tsp dill, finely chopped
1 tsp finely chopped fresh parsley
1 tsp finely chopped chives
juice of 1 lemon
seasoning

Heat the olive oil in a pan until warm, not hot. Remove from the heat and add the chopped tomato, chopped herbs, lemon juice and seasoning. Allow to infuse for 2 minutes before serving.

Parsley oil

bunch of flat leaf parsley
2 tsp walnuts (entirely optional, or substitute with what you have)
75ml extra virgin olive oil
pinch of salt

You will also need: stick blender with bowl attachment

Put all the ingredients into a blender bowl and blitz with a stick blender until smooth.

Basil oil

Uses: large bunch of basil, extra virgin olive oil, stick blender with bowl attachment

Drop the whole bunch of basil into boiling water for about 5 seconds. Remove with a slotted spoon and transfer to a bowl of ice-cold water. Keep the cold tap running over the basil in the bowl for 2 minutes, then remove and pat dry with kitchen paper. Put the basil leaves and oil into a stick blender bowl and blitz.

Chicken

I've given chicken its own section because it is by far the cheapest, most widely used and versatile meat and offers the best opportunity for saving money through multiple use. The price of chicken varies considerably, from cheap as chips for the intensively reared, water-injected kind to double figures for the free-as-a-bird organic specimens. I would suggest buying the best you can afford – and always try to buy a whole chicken. With a little practice you'll be able to joint it in minutes (see page 102), leaving with you with two breasts (complete with fillet and knuckle bone), two wings, two thighs, two drumsticks and a substantial carcass to boot for making a flavoursome stock. Of course, you've also got the option of leaving the chicken whole for roasting and poaching.

Tasty brown chicken stock

There is no substitute for the flavour of a home-made stock. It makes use not only of the carcass but also that old, bendy carrot, last bit of celery, etc. Worth the effort!

2 chicken carcasses
oil for frying
1 onion
1 carrot
1 leek
1 celery stick
half a garlic bulb
1 dsp tomato purée
1 bay leaf
sprig of fresh thyme
sprig of fresh rosemary

Preheat the oven to 200°C (Gas Mark 6). Heat a couple of tablespoons of oil in a large frying pan. Add the broken-up carcasses and wings (possibly in batches) and fry on a high heat until deep golden brown. Transfer to a roasting tray and bake in the oven for about 20 minutes.

Meanwhile, fry the veg in the same frying pan, using the chicken fat that's still in the pan. When the veg start to brown, add the tomato purée and stir for 1-2 minutes.

Combine the chicken carcasses, veg and herbs in a large pan and cover with cold water. Bring to the boil, skim off any fat, reduce the heat and simmer for at least 3 hours. Skim off any fat every now and again, and keep topped up with water if the bones become exposed.

Strain through a fine sieve, allow to cool, then divide into containers for batch freezing. The stock can be reduced until it darkens and thickens for a restaurant-style jus, or made into a gravy using thickening granules and any additional flavourings. Or simply use as a stock for soups and sauces.

Jointing a chicken

1. Place the chicken on its side. Lift the leg slightly and cut through to remove the leg and thigh. Turn it over and repeat. Remove the breasts from the carcass by cutting along the top of the breastbone, slightly to one side. Then, following the breastbone with the knife, free the flesh from the bone.

2. Repeat for the other breast.

3. Separate the wings from the breasts. Pull the wing away from the body then cut through the joint of the wing and breast.

You can now freeze all the parts separately. I usually wait till I've got two or three complete carcasses before turning them into stock.

Whole poached chicken

This is a great way to take advantage of one of those reduced-price offers when stuff is on or approaching its 'use by' date. You'll be eating chicken for lunch and dinner, but never the same way twice. The gentle poaching keeps in all that succulence that so easily gets lost through roasting, plus it's mega-healthy because you dispense with the skin. It's also a great way to use up those veg-rack lone losers. Just peel what needs peeling (that doesn't include onions – the skin is fine in the cooking liquor). Carrot, celery, fennel, garlic, leek and onion will all add fabulous flavour to the finished article.

Once you've allowed the chicken to cool in its poaching water, drain well, remove the skin and use your fingers to get every last scrap of meat off the bones, tearing it up into bite-sized pieces as you go along. (But try not to eat it all as you go along!) Make sure the white breast meat gets well combined with the tastier, darker leg meat. You'll be amazed how much it yields.

1 whole chicken
2 carrots
1 celery stick
1 onion
3 garlic cloves

Put the chicken and all the vegetables into a large pan. Cover completely with cold water and bring to the boil. Skim off any scum that rises to the top, then reduce the heat and simmer for 15 minutes. Remove from the heat and allow the chicken to cool in the poaching water.

Four poached chicken meals

★ Combine with a little mayo, chopped cooked green veg and/or tinned sweetcorn for a fab sandwich filling.
★ Use the same combo as above for an amazing composite salad.
★ Combine with a few sautéd mushrooms and a scattering of herbs for a mouth-watering omelette filling (page 42).
★ Chop into small pieces and mix with béchamel sauce (page 44) for an alternative cauliflower cheese dish (page 80).

One-pan spatchcocked roast chicken

Spatchcocked. Sounds technical, but it basically just involves cutting through the breastbone of the chicken then opening it out flat. Just do it carefully with a large, sharp-tipped heavy knife. This preparation method allows for quicker cooking and holds a marinade really well – and spreading the whole chicken over all the other ingredients does wonders for the infusion of vegetable flavours. Dried oregano and Italian mixed herbs work well, as does fresh oregano, rosemary and thyme.

This goes to show that a good roast doesn't have to take all day. In fact, after less than five minutes of chopping, you can deliver the entire result within an hour while doing precisely nothing. The leftovers can of course be re-heated but, better still, they're a filling for leftover roast dinner pasty (page 142), mini Yorkshire puds (page 35) or stuffed butternut squash (page 141). The veg combo is up to you.

a few garlic cloves, lightly smashed
dried herbs
seasoning
1 mug water, or white wine
olive oil

Preheat the oven to 200°C (Gas Mark 6).

Slice all the vegetables into pieces about 1cm thick and spread out in the bottom of a roasting tray. Sprinkle with dried herbs and seasoning. Add the water or wine.

Spatchcock the chicken (see above). Lay it, skin side up, on top of the vegetable medley, drizzle with a good slug of oil and season. Roast for about 40 minutes.

Remove from the oven and cover loosely with foil. Leave to rest for 5-10 minutes, allowing the chicken juices to mingle with the vegetables and all that lovely herby flavour. Personally, I then like to deposit the entire shebang in the middle of the table for everyone to dig in. I do the same even if I'm dining alone, knowing that I've got a great leftover party to come!

Serves 4

1 whole chicken
2 carrots
2 onions
1 leek
1 celery stick
2 courgettes
handful of new potatoes

Spicy marinated chicken breast

It's amazing what a dollop of plain yogurt and a sprinkling of assorted spices can do for the selling price of fresh meat in a supermarket. It takes me precisely five seconds and virtually no money to do exactly the same in the privacy of my own kitchen. This is one of those marinated dishes that works just as well with immediate cooking – you don't need to put the chicken aside for the flavour to be absorbed. The combination of spices I've suggested here is purely a guideline, as I've rarely used the same combination twice when making this meal. Perhaps the only permanent fixture is the turmeric, as it adds such an appetising colour as well as flavour. One of my favourite ways to serve this dish is on top of flatbread (page 55) with a side serving of couscous (page 125) and baked bean salsa (page 134).

Serves 2

2 chicken breasts, cut on the diagonal into strips
1 dsp plain yogurt
1 tsp lemon juice
1 tsp curry powder
½ tsp turmeric
½ tsp ground coriander
pinch of salt and pepper
oil for frying

To make the spicy marinade, blend all the ingredients except the chicken and the oil together in a bowl, then coat the chicken pieces in the marinade.

Heat a frying pan over a moderate heat for 30 seconds or so then add about 1 tbsp oil. Add the chicken pieces, fry for a few minutes until golden brown then turn. Remove from the heat when the chicken is just cooked through and serve.

For other recipe ideas for chicken, see:

Yorkshire puddings: five gourmet Yorkshire pudding fillings (leftover roast chicken dinner) (page 35)
Lettuce: five little gem lettuce boats (shredded poached chicken and shaved Parmesan) (page 128)
Composite salads: ideas for composite salads (poached chicken and roast meat) (page 131)
Leftover roast dinner pasty (page 142)
Leftover roast chicken dinner stuffed squash (page 141)
Chicken and pea biryani (page 146)

Other meat and fish

I tend to accumulate much of my meat and fish when it's been substantially reduced in the supermarket due to being close to or having reached its 'use by' date. This is a fabulous way to buy a quality of produce you may not otherwise be able to afford. It's brilliant – free range, organic sausages for the price of intensively reared! You then have the choice of same-day cooking and then freezing (just be sure to mark it to eat immediately after defrosting), or eating straight away. A combination of this reduced-price produce with the remnants of your veg rack and contents of the old scary cupboard and you've got gourmet meals for bargain-basement prices.

Slow-roast pork belly

The only way to cook pork belly is long and slow. Not only does this make it melt-in-the-mouth tender, it also lends itself perfectly to the addition of a robust Belgian or English ale, which has time to really penetrate and flavour the meat. This is such a gloriously rustic dish that it requires minimum presentation. So rather than try to turn it into something fancy, just stick a huge bowl of mash in the middle of the table, pile the slices of pork on a big chopping board, pour the sauce and veg into a bowl with a ladle, and let your guests pile in.

Serves 4

1kg pork belly, preferably on the bone
2 carrots
1 celery stick
1 onion
3 garlic cloves
1 leek
330ml beer
1 tin chopped tomatoes
half a chicken stock cube, dissolved in 300ml water
1 bay leaf
3 sprigs rosemary

For the dry marinade:
1 dsp chopped fresh oregano
1 dsp chopped fresh parsley
1 dsp chopped fresh rosemary
1 garlic clove, finely chopped
1 heaped tsp sea salt
freshly ground black pepper

Preheat the oven to 150°C (Gas Mark 2).

Score the skin of the pork belly with a series of criss-cross slashes. You will need a Stanley knife, or an artist's scalpel (or, preferably, get your butcher to do it). Combine all the dry marinade ingredients then rub into the skin, as if you're giving a massage!

Chop the vegetables and put in the bottom of a roasting tin big enough to accommodate the pork belly. Place the pork belly on top of the veg then pour in the beer and the tomatoes. Add the stock until it reaches about two-thirds of the way up the sides of the meat. Add the herbs and roast in the oven for about 3½ hours.

Remove from the oven and set aside to rest for no less than 15 minutes. This allows the meat juices to flow into the sauce, giving added flavour.

Transfer the pork belly on to a chopping board. With a sharp knife, carefully cut the whole slab of meat away from the ribs. Then pull and cut away the crackling and set aside for garnish. If it's not crispy enough, return it to the oven and cook at 200°C (Gas Mark 6) for about 10 minutes, or until it's golden and crispy.

To serve, carve the meat into slices. See page 144 to find out what do with the leftovers.

Turkey burgers with non-pesto new potatoes, little gem lettuce and tomato salad

The inspiration for this recipe all started with a packet of defrosted free-range turkey mince that I'd grabbed because it had a bargain-busting 'reduced' sticker. It had top-tasting burgers written all over it. After a minute of chin rubbing, I fancied chucking in some finely chopped onion and fresh thyme. Unfortunately, a quick check of the veg rack yielded no onion, or thyme, but the fridge salad drawer did reveal some coriander (at least a week and a half old, but the damp kitchen paper and cling film trick had done its work). A further foray dug up a ripe tomato, half a roast garlic bulb and a few spoonfuls of non-pesto I'd salvaged from my cooking demo the weekend before. A tired old little gem lettuce revealed surprisingly crisp green leaves once I'd got rid of the browning outer ones, while a handful of about-to-turn new potatoes inspired a non-pesto potato salad. The rest was a simple case of assembly . . . Delish!

Spicy lamb burgers

There are home-made burgers, and then there are these flavour-packed exotic parcels. The aubergine pickle on page 67 is the perfect condiment for these and cuts through the minced lamb like a knife through butter. Feel free to play around with your own special spice mix, using whatever you have in the scary cupboard. If you're not sure about the amount of seasoning, fry a teaspoon of the mixture and taste.

Makes 4 x 250g burgers

For the burgers:
3 tbsp oil for frying
1 onion, finely chopped
1 tbsp ground cumin
1 tbsp ground coriander
½ tsp chilli flakes
1kg minced lamb
seasoning to taste

To serve:
4 slices halloumi cheese
4 bread buns
mixed-leaf salad of your choice
tomato slices
aubergine pickle (best served at room temperature)

Heat 1 tbsp oil in a frying pan and gently fry the onion for 2 minutes. Add the cumin, coriander and chilli flakes and fry for a further 2 minutes. Allow to cool.

Place the lamb mince in a mixing bowl then add the fried onion and spices, and salt and black pepper to taste. Combine well then divide the burger mixture into two and shape into equal-sized patties. There's no substitute for getting your hands messy here!

Heat the remaining oil in the same frying pan and fry the patties on a medium heat for about 5 minutes on each side, or until cooked through (although you can serve rare if you wish).

Preheat the grill to hot. Top the burgers with the halloumi slices and cook under the grill for 4-5 minutes, or until the cheese starts to go soft and brown.

While the burgers are grilling, cut the bread buns in half and, gently fry the cut sides in the same frying pan until lightly browned, adding a little more oil if required.

To serve, arrange salad leaves and tomato slices on the bottom half of each bun, then place the burger and other bun half on top. Serve with aubergine pickle on the side.

Smoked chunky beef chilli

I always buy reduced packets of minced beef and get them straight into the freezer, or cook a huge batch of chilli and then freeze it in portions. Remember you can freeze, cook and then freeze again – as long as you've changed the state of the original food. You can play around with the chilli element to suit your own taste. Remember that the seeds are the hottest part of the chilli.

Makes 6 good-sized bowls

oil for frying
300g braising steak, cut into small cubes, approximately 1cm square
500g minced beef
1 onion, finely chopped
2 garlic cloves, crushed
30g red chillies, finely chopped
½ tsp chilli powder
1 tsp smoked paprika
1 dsp tomato purée
1 tin chopped tomatoes
1 tin kidney beans, drained
seasoning

Heat a little oil in a large pan and fry the braising steak until it browns. Remove from the pan and set aside. Brown the mince in the same pan, and set aside with the braising steak, including any meat juices.

Add a little oil to the pan then fry the onion, crushed garlic and chopped chillies for a few minutes until they start to soften. Add the chilli powder and paprika and continue to fry for a further 2 minutes, stirring continuously so that the mixture doesn't burn in the bottom of the pan. Add the tomato purée and fry for 2 minutes more, stirring as it cooks.

Return the meat and juices to the pan along with the tinned tomatoes and simmer very gently for at least 1½ hours. About 15 minutes before the end of cooking, add the drained kidney beans and seasoning.

Lamb tagine skewers

A traditional Moroccan tagine infused with honey and lemon is one of my all-time favourite dishes to cook and eat – the amazing taste is well worth the effort. Bursting with fragrant herbs and spices, and a balance of sweetness and acidity, this barbecue version captures all the classic elements. It'll clear out your scary cupboard, and works with almost any cut of lamb. Dig into the freezer for one of those supermarket bargains, or treat yourself from your local butcher.

Makes 4 skewers

For the marinade:
1 onion, finely chopped
2 garlic cloves, crushed or finely chopped
1 tsp turmeric
1 tsp cinnamon
1 tsp ground coriander
1 tsp ground ginger
juice and zest of 1 lemon
1 tsp honey
40ml olive oil

400g lamb neck fillet, trimmed and cut into 2½cm cubes
1 aubergine, cut into 2½cm cubes
1 onion

You will also need: 4 long skewers (if they're wooden, soak in water before using)

To make the marinade, heat a little oil in a large frying pan, add the onion and garlic and gently cook until soft. Add the turmeric, cinnamon, coriander and ginger and fry, stirring regularly, for 2 minutes. Add the lemon juice, keeping a little in reserve, and the honey and 40ml olive oil and saffron.

Lay the lamb in a ceramic dish and coat with the marinade. Cover and refrigerate and leave to marinate, ideally overnight.

Fire up the barbecue, or pre-heat a ribbed griddle pan. Cut the aubergine into 2½cm cubes and squeeze over a little lemon juice to prevent discolouration. Peel the onion and cut into quarters, then separate each quarter into its individual layers.

To assemble the skewers, alternate the lamb and aubergine cubes, making sure you've got a piece of onion or two between them.

Place the lamb skewers on the barbecue or in a griddle pan and cook over a high heat for a few minutes on each side.

Sausage casserole

This winter-warming comfort fodder packs a serious flavour punch with just these limited ingredients. But have a swift check of the veg rack and the fridge before you start because it will happily accommodate chunky bits of carrot, leek, mushrooms and/or celery, as well as bacon and any other meat and veg. And of course you can throw in a sprig or two of fresh oregano, rosemary or thyme along with, or instead of, the dried herbs. If you're adding cooked leftovers, wait until about 10 minutes before the end of cooking time; if adding raw ingredients, throw them in as you fry the sausage and onion. Serve with pasta, rice, baked potato or simply on its own with chunks of crusty bread to mop up.

Serves 3-4

4 tbsp oil for frying
500g sausages, cut into bite-sized pieces
1 onion, sliced
500ml stock
1 tsp dried mixed herbs
500g waxy new potatoes, sliced a little thicker than a £1 coin

Preheat the oven to 200°C (Gas Mark 6).

Heat the oil in a heavy-based, ovenproof saucepan or casserole dish. Add the sausage pieces and onion and fry for 5 minutes.

Add the stock and the herbs then bring to a simmer. Add the potatoes and put in the oven for 30-45 minutes, depending on how thick you want the stock (it gradually reduces and thickens during cooking).

Whole baked bream on roasted veg

A good meaty fish such as bream is ideal for this whole baked dish. Black bream is a real favourite of mine. It's cheap and readily available in supermarkets, it's on the sustainable fish list and it's got fabulous firm flesh that stands up to the big roasted flavours of the vegetable medley. Just be sure to ask your supplier to scale, gut and clean the fish. Any roast veg can be used here, but fennel is superb with fish and you've got the added bonus of the fronds, which you can use to stuff the fish along with the herbs. It's a brilliant dinner-party dish as the veg can be cooked ahead of time, then all you need to do is plonk the fish on top, roast and serve the whole caboodle as a one-pot dish for everyone to dive into.

Serves 3-4

a full serving of assorted roast vegetables (page 63)
3 whole fish such as black bream, scaled, gutted and cleaned
seasoning
a large handful of assorted fresh fine herbs, roughly chopped (including the chopped fennel fronds)
juice of 1 lemon; reserve the remaining lemon pieces
1 large glass white wine

Preheat the oven to 180°C (Gas Mark 4).

Spread the cooled or refrigerated roast vegetables in a roasting tray big enough to accommodate the fish.

Make 3 or 4 diagonal incisions on each side of the fish. Season the cavity of each fish with salt and pepper and then stuff with the herbs.

Lay the fish on top of the vegetables. Pour over the lemon juice and place the reserved lemon pieces in the roasting tray.

Tip in the wine, put the tray in the preheated oven and roast for about 25 minutes, or until the fish is just cooked through.

Remove from the oven and serve immediately – preferably in its roasting dish straight from the oven.

Kedgeree fishcakes

My all-time favourite fishcake recipe! The poached-egg topping and the sauce vierge turn this into gastro-pub heaven in your own home. Try adding cooked peas or shredded spinach leaves to the fishcake mix for even more colour and flavour.

Makes 2 fishcakes

oil for frying
half an onion, finely chopped
½ tsp turmeric
½ tsp curry powder
100g basmati rice
200ml water
200g smoked haddock, preferably undyed
1 medium-sized potato (Maris Piper or similar), peeled, quartered, boiled and mashed
seasoning
2 tbsp flour
2 eggs, beaten
2 tbsp breadcrumbs

To serve:
2 poached eggs
2 tbsp sauce vierge (page 99)

Heat 1 tbsp oil in a lidded frying pan and gently fry the onion over a medium heat for a few minutes until soft. Add the turmeric and curry powder and fry for a further minute. Set aside and allow to cool for a few minutes.

Add the rice to the frying pan and stir to coat in the onion and spices, then pour over the water and return to the heat. Bring to the boil with a lid on, reduce to a simmer and cook for 7 minutes. Turn off the heat and allow to stand, covered, for a further 7 minutes.

Meanwhile, cook the smoked haddock. Fill a small pan with enough cold water to cover the haddock. Bring to the boil, add the haddock, then reduce the heat to a simmer and cook for 3 minutes. Remove the haddock from the pan and flake into a large bowl.

Combine the cooked rice and mash with the smoked haddock flakes and season to taste. Shape the mixture into two patties.

Place the flour in one bowl, the beaten egg in another and the breadcrumbs in a third. Carefully dip each patty in the flour, patting off any excess, then in the egg and then in the breadcrumbs.

Heat 1 tbsp oil in a frying pan and cook the fishcakes for a few minutes on both sides until golden brown and heated through. To serve, top each with a poached egg and spoon around the sauce vierge.

Bacon-wrapped fish finger parcel on toast with pea purée

This has to be the ultimate way to serve bacon, eggs and fish fingers. It's not often that I would advocate a surf-and-turf combo, but fish such as cod, monkfish and scallops are classically accompanied by pancetta or bacon.

Makes 1 luxury open sarni

3 thin slices back bacon, or 6 slices streaky
3 fish fingers
half a mug frozen peas
1 egg
oil for frying
1 slice toast

You will also need: stick blender

Preheat the oven to 200°C (Gas Mark 6). Lay the slices of bacon on a baking tray, slightly overlapping. Put the fish fingers on to the bacon and wrap up in a parcel. Bake in the oven for 15 minutes.

Meanwhile, bring a pan of water or veg stock to the boil and cook the peas for about 5 minutes. Drain, reserving 4 tbsp of boiling liquid. Add the reserved liquid to the peas and blitz with a stick blender. Gently fry the egg.

To serve, put the bacon and fish finger parcel on the slice of toast. Top with the fried egg with the pea purée on the side.

For other recipe ideas for meat and fish, see:

Whatever-you-want flan (page 40)
Perfect omelette: five omelette fillings (smoked haddock) (page 42)
Baked eggs (page 43)
White sauce (page 44)
Welsh rarebit: four Welsh rarebit meals (smoked haddock) (page 49)
Flatbread (page 55)
Smoked haddock cauliflower cheese on chargrilled baguette (page 80)
Potato *Rösti* (page 93)
Composite salads: ideas for composite salads (bacon – grilled, baked or fried and chopped) (page 131)
Slow-roast pork belly, apple sauce and black pudding bruschetta (page 144)
Sausage, courgettes and peas in tomato sauce (page 145)

Pasta, rice, couscous and pulses

Rice and especially pulses often induce fear and trepidation for no good reason. If you can make a cup of tea, then you can get to grips with these innocuous little packets and unleash a whole new repertoire of flavour-packed possibilities. In this chapter I describe the basic techniques for cooking pasta, rice, couscous and lentils, then show how these can be combined with foods from the fridge, veg rack and scary cupboard to create an endless variety of dishes.

Pasta

There's probably nothing new I can tell you about the joy of eating a huge bowl of perfectly cooked pasta coated with a fabulous creamy carbonara, herby tomato or chilli- and garlic-infused sauce. With a packet of dried pasta in the cupboard, you will rarely be at a loss for a quick and tasty meal. This is partly why I avoid buying the fresh stuff. Not only does it have a premium price tag and a short shelf life compared with dried, but I reckon it's not as tasty as good-quality dried pasta.

When illustrating the benefits of cooking and chilling your veg and combining random bits of cooked leftovers, I will always refer to pasta. On average it takes about 10 minutes to cook pasta until al dente in salted boiling water. Once drained it can be returned to the pan with any number of bits from the fridge and warmed through over a low heat.

Invariably you will cook too much (don't worry, everyone does). Simply set aside the excess and, while still warm, add a slug of olive oil – just enough for a light coating when mixed in. This will stop it congealing into a useless pasta brick. Spread it out in a thin layer to cool quickly and evenly (remember residual heat will always continue the cooking process well after you've removed the food from the heat source).

Cheese and tuna pasta
Uses: pasta, tinned tuna, cream cheese, peas

This is one of my favourite quick-fix lunch or dinner dishes. It takes around 10 minutes to cook the pasta, plus 2 minutes for stirring in the other ingredients, and leftovers can be cooled and refrigerated for a tasty, instant lunch for days to come. Every ingredient here is interchangeable – apart from the pasta, although the type of pasta could be anything. Try substituting tuna with salmon (tinned or flaked fresh), cream cheese with crème fraîche, and peas with broccoli or chargrilled courgettes. Feel free to keep me updated with your favourite combos through Facebook.

Three key pasta sauces

★ Cream-based sauce: Melt your choice of cheese in seasoned cream or crème fraîche, along with any other cooked ingredients you want to add. Then pour over hot pasta, or over cold pasta and then heat through in a saucepan over a low heat.

★ Olive oil-based sauce: Heat the olive oil over a low heat for 2 minutes until warm, not hot, then add flavourings such as finely chopped chillies, garlic, anchovies, etc., before stirring into hot, drained pasta.

★ Tomato-based sauce (page 97): Add any selection of pre-cooked ingredients (broccoli, chargrilled courgette, peas, shredded roast chicken or sliced sausage) to this tomato sauce, then heat through before adding to pasta. If the pasta is pre-cooked and straight from the fridge, combine all the ingredients - sauce and all - in one pan and heat, stirring regularly, until hot enough to serve.

NOTE: A ladle or two of the salted water used for cooking the pasta can be added to a sauce for extra flavour and saucy consistency.

Rice

Rice can be divided into two main types: long-grain and starchy short-grain. Long-grain rice such as basmati is generally used for Indian-style dishes. Short-grain varieties such as Italian arborio or Spanish bomba are more suited to risotto and paella, Californian and Japanese varieties are best for sushi, while Thai fragrant rice is good for sticky rice. But for the sake of simplicity and common use, we'll just focus on long-grain and Italian short-grain rice.

Long-grain rice

Pop the rice into a pan, stir in double the volume of water or stock and a pinch of salt. Put a lid on, bring to the boil then reduce the heat. Simmer for 7 minutes, then turn off the heat and keep covered for a further 7 minutes before fluffing up with a fork. Once you've embraced this simple technique, you can start experimenting by frying a base of onions then adding chopped and cooked veg before adding the rice and following the same cooking method. See the leftover biryani dish (page 146).

Short-grain rice (basic risotto)

To make risotto, bring vegetable or chicken stock to the boil, then reduce the heat and simmer. Gently fry some finely diced onion, garlic and herbs in a heavy-bottomed pan. Add the rice, stir and then start adding the stock a couple of ladles at a time, stirring constantly. Allow the stock to be fully absorbed by the rice before adding the next couple of ladles. Continue to add stock until the rice is al dente, about 15-20 minutes. Add any extra flavours, such as cheese, purées or cooked vegetables, to the pan about 2 minutes before serving.

Top three rice dishes

* Butternut squash and goat's cheese risotto (page 73)
* Kedgeree fishcakes (page 116)
* Chicken and pea biryani (page 146) - pictured above

A special note on cooling and re-heating rice Rice carries a reputation for being the bad boy of the cook-and-chill principle - and for good reason. The bacteria that can cause food poisoning don't get killed off through normal boiling and steaming. However, re-heating rice once is fine, providing you cooled and stored it properly beforehand. As soon as it's cooked, spread it out thinly on a large plate or tray to allow for quick and even cooling. Once cool, immediately put it into an airtight container and store in the fridge until needed. It will keep for 2-3 days. The same cooling method also applies to pasta and couscous.

Lentils

Lentils are cooked in a similar way to rice. You can create a tasty dish by just simmering them, but you can do a whole lot more by adding flavour enhancers, from finely diced carrot, onion and celery to chopped bacon or pancetta. Bear in mind that differently coloured lentils require different cooking times, so refer to the instructions on the packet.

Smoked veggie chilli pie

This is one of those mate's mum's recipes you tend to hear about while on the subject of food. It's hugely adaptable. If you're pushed for time, you don't have to include the mash topping or bake it in the oven – it's a perfectly good veggie chilli as is. You can also use any combo of tinned beans you have – including baked beans. Serve it with crusty bread, roast potato wedges or a big bag of tortilla chips.

Serves 4

600g potatoes, peeled and cut into large, even-sized chunks

200g green or brown lentils

150ml water or stock

2 tbsp olive oil for frying

2 onions, finely sliced

2 cloves garlic, crushed

½ tsp chilli powder

1 tsp smoked paprika

2 tbsp tomato purée

1 tbsp Worcester sauce

1 tin chopped tomatoes

1 tin kidney beans, drained

1 tin butter beans, drained

You will also need: potato ricer or masher

Preheat the oven to 180°C (Gas Mark 4). First, prepare the mash. Put the potatoes into a pan of cold salted water. Bring to the boil and then simmer until the potatoes are cooked through. Drain well and mash using, ideally, a potato ricer.

Put the lentils in a frying pan over a low heat, pour over the water or stock and top up with water to cover. Bring to the boil and simmer for about 20 minutes, or until tender.

Heat the oil in a large saucepan and cook the onions and garlic until soft but without colour. Add the chilli powder and smoked paprika and cook for another 2 minutes. Add the tomato purée and cook, stirring regularly to avoid burning, for 2 minutes more. Add the lentils plus all the remaining ingredients except the potatoes, and mix well.

Put into an ovenproof dish and cover with the mash, then bake for 30 minutes.

Couscous

Couscous is a cinch to cook: just put it into a bowl or pan, add an equal amount of boiling water or vegetable stock, cover and leave to stand off the heat for 10 minutes. Job done! You've got an accompaniment to big-flavoured dishes such as tagines, or the basis for a salad.

Top-tasting couscous

While plain cooked couscous is ultra quick and perfect for accompanying flavoursome dishes such as tagines, couscous can make a fabulous stand-alone meal in its own right. I like to think of this as a self-evolving dish that continually changes throughout the week as you add bits and pieces of appetising leftovers.

oil for frying
1 onion, finely chopped
3 garlic cloves, crushed
1 tsp ground cumin
1 mug couscous
zest of 1 lemon
1 mug water or stock
1 mug frozen peas
1 tbsp finely chopped fresh coriander
seasoning
slug of olive oil

Heat 1 tbsp oil in a saucepan over a medium heat and gently fry the onion and garlic until soft, but without colour.

Add the cumin powder and cook for a further minute, stirring constantly. Add the couscous, lemon zest and boiling water or stock. Give a quick stir, put on a tight-fitting lid and remove from the heat.

Leave to stand for 10 minutes and then add the peas and chopped coriander, stir in well and put the lid back on for a further 2 minutes. Transfer the couscous to a bowl or container and fluff up with a fork. Add seasoning to taste, and the olive oil.

For other recipe ideas for pasta, rice, couscous and pulses, see:

Rich tomato passata (page 97)
Hey pesto: four good uses for hey pesto (hey pesto sauce – pasta) (page 130)

The salad drawer

I've witnessed my share of horrific salad-drawer sights in my time – not least in my own fridge. As with other fruit and veg, much of this decay and waste is caused by a desire to eat more healthily, which is quickly overridden by our body's innate urge for fat and flavour. I'm certainly not going to preach about rabbit food, but I am going to give you ideas for how to get the best out of these tricky customers.

Here's a scary statistic for you: we throw away 50p in £1 of a bagged salad.* Of course we do. Open the bag and before you can say "pass the dressing" the whole lot has withered to a limp mess. As with fragile herbs (see page 98), the secret is to remove the salad from its packaging and transfer it to a container lined with kitchen paper or an unused J cloth. Fold the paper or cloth over the salad, dampen with cold water, then cover with a lid or cling film and store in the fridge. Really – it works!

* From 'Household food and drink waste in the UK, November 2009', WRAP

Lettuce

I tend to go for little gem lettuce as it seems to last longer than others. And, contrary to popular belief, a few brown leaves on the outside doesn't mean the entire thing is polluted. Just remove them to find a tight bundle of pristine green leaves below. Little gem is also more versatile: you can braise it as a vegetable accompaniment or use the smaller inner leaves as mini boat-style holding vessels for cold finger food.

Five little gem lettuce boats

★ Poached salmon, lemon crème fraîche and dill – pictured below
★ Shredded poached chicken and shaved Parmesan
★ Tuna mayo, chopped green beans and capers
★ Leftover biryani (see page 146) mixed with a little mayonnaise, sultanas and toasted flaked almonds

Celery

Celery Right, who's ever used an entire head of celery?! I suppose there are very good economic reasons for not selling individual celery sticks. Good reasons for the producers and retailers, that is, not us poor fools who have to buy a pile of stuff we don't need – never mind the space a whole head takes up in the salad drawer. Of the entire veg rack and salad drawer suspects, the dastardly celery gave me the biggest challenge to find something scrummy to make out of a whole head in one go. The good news is, I have!

Braised celery with Stilton and walnut crust

Apparently, you use more calories eating celery than there are in it, so I thought I'd better throw in the blue cheese to redress such an absurd balance! I love this dish, not only because it uses a whole bunch of celery but because it transforms something that in its raw form can be, well, too boring and celery-like, into smooth and luscious comfort food.

Serves 2

1 head of celery, cut in half
1 litre chicken or vegetable stock
3 tbsp cream cheese
1 tbsp walnuts
2 tbsp breadcrumbs
1 big tbsp Stilton

You will also need: stick blender with bowl attachment or food processor

Preheat the oven to 180°C (Gas Mark 4).

Place the celery and 850ml stock in a saucepan and simmer for 30 minutes.

Meanwhile, mix 150ml warm stock with the cream cheese.

Remove the celery from the heat, allow it to cool and then roughly chop. Combine with the cream cheese and stock mix and transfer to an ovenproof serving dish.

Blitz the walnuts using a stick blender with bowl attachment, then add the breadcrumbs and cheese, and pulse for a few seconds until fully combined. Cover the celery with the topping and bake in the preheated oven for 10-15 minutes, until the topping is brown.

Hey pesto!

Basil, pine nuts and Parmesan. If you've always got these on hand, then you've no need for this book! I love a classic Italian pesto as much as anyone, but I've created substantial volumes of equally tasty pesto for a fraction of the price. Basically, if it's green and grows; cheesy and crumbly; brown and nutty, you're in business. Just add seasoning and a slug of oil then stick it in the fridge or freezer or tuck straight in. Those seemingly insignificant leftovers are ideal candidates for this: boiled broccoli florets, cooked peas or broad beans. And that bought-in-the-bag combo of rocket, spinach and watercress makes the most vibrant green sauce.

a big handful of mixed green leaves (such as rocket, spinach and watercress)
1 large thumb-sized piece of cheese (such as Cheddar)
1 dsp nuts (any will do)
1 garlic clove, crushed (or a squeeze of roasted garlic – page 83)
50ml extra virgin olive oil
seasoning to taste

You will also need: stick blender with bowl attachment or food processor

Whizz up all the ingredients until the desired consistency. Just remember, *you can add but you can't take away* . . . Taste and adjust! You can get a drizzling sauce consistency by adding more oil, or a firmer dip by using less oil. The choice is yours.

Four good uses for hey pesto

★ Hey pesto canapés: pile finely chopped leftover roasted or chargrilled veg on crostini and top with hey pesto.
★ Hey pesto crème fraîche: add crème fraîche and gently heat for a creamy sauce with chicken and pasta.
★ Hey pesto dip: serve in a bowl with flatbread or crostini.
★ Hey pesto sauce: add more oil to the pesto for a pouring consistency. Makes a lovely pasta sauce or a tasty addition to cooked fish and veg.

Composite salads

Salad gets a bit of a raw deal as a food choice, tending to be seen as more punishment than pleasure, but healthy food doesn't have to be this way. As soon as you move away from thinking that salads have to contain merely salad and embrace the composite salad concept, you're on to winning combos. Composite salads are one of the best ways to use up random cooked leftovers to maximum effect. Some of the most famous salad dishes were products of the 'use what you have to hand' principle: Caesar salad, for example, was invented by the Italian–American chef and restaurateur Caesar Cardini, apparently after a particularly busy 4 July depleted his kitchen supplies.

Composite salad ideas – just mix and match

Just chop, flake or slice the following in any combo you fancy:

★ Bacon - grilled, baked or fried and chopped
★ Broad beans - boiled
★ Button mushrooms - sliced and sautéd
★ Eggs (quail's eggs are fabulous - boil for 2 1/2 minutes, refresh under cold water and peel)
★ Green beans - boiled and sliced
★ New potatoes - roast and halved or sliced and boiled
★ Peas
★ Roast meat
★ Sausage - cooked and sliced
★ Seared tuna
★ Tinned salmon
★ Tinned tuna
★ Toasted pine nuts
★ Crostini (page 54)
★ Courgettes - chargrilled and sliced (page 81)
★ Flat-cap mushrooms - baked and sliced (page 84)
★ Roasted red pepper - peeled and sliced in strips (page 94)
★ Poached chicken (page 103)

Tin can alley

When looking for gastronomic inspiration, the tin can alley of your downtown kitchen cupboard may not be your first-choice destination. But I guarantee that it plays host to the most eclectic mix of fish, pulses and vegetables to give you anything from a Moroccan chickpea-based roast to a range of home-made dips and sauces you'll never be lucky enough to grab from the supermarket shelves. Just dig out the remnants of the roast garlic, the last spoonful of Philly from the fridge and that half a dried-out lemon, left behind after the vodka and tonic ran out, and tin can alley becomes an Aladdin's cave of savoury delights.

Baked bean salsa

Sounds bizarre, but by George it works! And what a way to use up those last two spoonfuls of beans (not to mention that red pepper remnant that's starting to curl up at the sides).

2 dsp baked beans
quarter of a red pepper
pinch of chilli flakes
pinch of salt and pepper
1 tsp lime juice
1 tsp chopped fresh coriander

You will also need: stick blender with bowl attachment

Pulse the beans and red pepper using a stick blender, then combine with the other ingredients and chill.

Houmous

Why buy this favourite classic when you can make it in minutes for a fraction of the price? The only unfamiliar ingredient here might be tahini (sesame seed paste). It's available in most supermarkets, but you can still make a pretty tasty version without it.

1 tin chickpeas, drained and rinsed
juice of half a lemon
1 tsp tahini (optional)
½ tsp ground cumin
1-2 garlic cloves, crushed
60ml extra virgin olive oil
seasoning to taste

You will also need: food processor

Simply combine all the ingredients using a food processor to form a smooth and creamy dip.

Fish finger, tuna mayo and broccoli fishcakes

This recipe is purely a guideline, as you can substitute practically every ingredient with anything similar you might have lying around. Experiment with different leftovers and you'll end up with your own signature fishcake to make Findus green with envy. For a colourful accompaniment, try the sauce vierge on page 99.

To make an exotic Thai version without broccoli, substitute tinned salmon for tuna mayo, coriander for parsley, lime for lemon juice – plus the zest of one lime – and a little slug of sweet chilli sauce. Swapping continents has never been so easy.

Makes 2 fishcakes

2 cooked fish fingers, roughly chopped
2 tbsp tuna mayonnaise
1 dsp chopped fresh parsley
juice of half a lemon
2 tbsp mashed potato
2 cooked broccoli florets, chopped
1 tsp tomato ketchup
seasoning to taste
oil for frying
1 tbsp plain flour (seasoned)
1 egg, beaten
2 tbsp breadcrumbs

Preheat the oven to 180°C (Gas Mark 4).

Combine the fishcake ingredients in a bowl and shape into 2 patties.

Place the flour in one bowl, the beaten egg in another and the breadcrumbs in a third. Coat each patty in the flour, patting off any excess, then the egg wash and finally the breadcrumbs.

Fry in oil for 2 minutes on each side until golden brown and then finish the patties in the preheated oven for 10 minutes until warmed through.

Kidney bean and blue cheese dip

The essence of this fabulous dip is cream cheese and tinned beans. The rest is down to your taste and available ingredients. Cream cheese gives a smooth base for any other cheese you've got lurking in the fridge, while any type of bean will do (aduki, cannellini, butter beans . . .). Lemon juice and garlic are optional, and you can add a range of herbs for more flavour. Served with home-made flatbread, this is perfect party finger food.

Serves 2 as a starter

1 tin red kidney beans, drained and rinsed
2 dsp cream cheese
2 dsp blue cheese
squeeze of lemon juice (optional)
squeeze of roast garlic (optional)
(page 83)

You will also need: stick blender with bowl attachment or food processor

Blend all the ingredients using a stick blender or a food processor and serve with flatbread (page 55).

For other recipe ideas for tinned food, see:

Change your thinking: salsatastic! (carrot and kidney bean) (page 17)
Egg, anchovy and roast pepper bruschetta (tinned tuna) (page 39)
Perfect omelette: five omelette fillings (grated cheese and tinned tuna) (page 42)
Stuffed jacket potato: four luxury fillings for jacket potato (baked beans and tinned salmon) (page 87)
Stuffed red pepper tuna melts (page 95)
Cheese and tuna pasta (page 121)
Smoked veggie chilli pie (kidney beans) (page 124)
Composite salads: ideas for composite salads (tinned salmon and tinned tuna) (page 131)

Cooked leftovers

For the purposes of this book, I'm classifying cooked leftovers separately from food you've cooked specifically to refrigerate or freeze, as they tend to be random bits and pieces as opposed to portion-sized meals. Cooked leftovers can be anything from Sunday lunch remnants, such as a couple of roast potatoes, a floret of boiled broccoli, a rogue fish finger that didn't fit into the fish finger sarnie, fried bacon, sausage, a few green beans, leftover takeaway . . . In other words, anything you cooked to eat but didn't finish. If you've got a dog, you won't be wasting this kind of produce and your beloved pooch will be eating like a king. The reasons why cooked leftovers often end up in the bin is first because they don't look particularly appetising and second because their portion value gets overlooked: a floret of broccoli, a couple of tablespoons of peas, a rasher of bacon, half a sausage . . . The list is endless – and it all adds up to a few quid and one heck of a lot of combined flavour.

So what's the solution? Take lots of random morsels and combine them to make a whole new meal – packed into a pasty, for example, or added to rice as a biryani. Alternatively, you can turn a couple of spoonfuls into hot and cold light bites. Mash them together into a pâté, stuff them into tomatoes and bake, or serve them on/in

little edible vessels such as bruschetta and mini bread tart cases. Mini Yorkshire puddings (page 35), crostini (page 54), stuffed cabbage leaves (page 74) and lettuce boats (page 128) also make fantastic edible vessels. My ideas for these almost-free canapés and finger foods were very much inspired by Spanish tapas, traditionally served free with drinks in bars and bodegas. After years of travelling and living in the country, I developed a real love for these delicious appetisers, which mix everyday ingredients and leftovers in simple but imaginative ways.

Nacho pâté

Talk about a culinary metamorphosis: a couple of spoonfuls of congealed leftovers transformed into lip-smacking dip in seconds! I can recall looking at the leftover cheesy nachos on the plate and realising that re-heating in any form just wouldn't work. Blitzing was the only way forwards, and even then I wasn't convinced it would taste OK. Sure, the combo of tortillas, jalapeños, sour cream and cheese  obviously made sense, based on the original dish, but cold and combined? It was a case of suck it and see. Well, it was a revelation. And if I ever see this packaged as a ready-made supermarket dip, I shall be contacting my lawyers!

Leftover roast chicken dinner stuffed squash

Uses: 1 whole roasted butternut squash (page 71), knob of butter (about 50g), roast chicken dinner leftovers, grated cheese

This squash-stuffing concept will work beautifully with any roast dinner leftovers. After roasting the squash (see page 71), dig out the flesh and mix with a good knob of butter and lots of black pepper for the topping. Stuff the squash with roast dinner leftovers, top with the squash flesh and grate over a good chunk of cheese. For the stuffing I used the chicken I'd scraped off the carcass after jointing (see page 102), a bowl of roast chicken bits and a couple of spoonfuls of vegetable gravy – then scattered the whole lot with Parmesan. What a result!

Leftover roast dinner pasty

This is so good it could become a star performer in its own right. Think about it – all those irresistible roast dinner remnants, neatly repackaged in one big pasty . . . Love it! This particular pasty included roast chicken thigh meat, about three chunks of carrot, a floret of broccoli, a floret of cauliflower cheese and roast potato, all chopped up and bound together by three tablespoons of onion gravy.

Makes 1 large pasty

flour for dusting
250g shortcrust pastry (page 40)
enough leftovers to fill a pasty when chopped and combined together
a little milk or beaten egg (optional)
leftover gravy

Preheat the oven to 200°C (Gas Mark 6).

Dust the work surface with flour and roll out the pastry to about 3mm thick. Take a plate, saucer or any kind of disc template about 19cm in diameter, place on the pastry and cut around. Ball up the excess pastry, wrap in cling film and freeze for a later date.

Place the combined leftover mix on one half of the pastry disc, leaving a good 1cm border. Brush the edge with a little water, fold over and seal by pressing down with your thumb all the way round.

Brush the pasty with more water, milk or beaten egg, place on an oiled baking tray and bake in the preheated oven for 30 minutes. Serve with a jug of leftover gravy on the side.

Instant tortilla pizza

This is one of my favourite live demonstration dishes to get non-cooks and especially students to embrace the concept of transforming tired, unexciting produce into top-tasting tucker. It seems nearly everyone has a packet of those ready-made flour tortillas in the cupboard or fridge, and more often than not the packet is open and the tortillas are drying out. Well, that's no problem for this recipe.

What's more, this is quicker to make than waiting for a pizza to be delivered – and it's cheaper too. An average takeaway/delivery will cost you eight quid for a normal-sized pizza, but this home-made version is practically free. It can be made with cooked leftovers or past-it veg that needs using up – either can go straight on to the pizza; only mushrooms need to be pre-cooked first. Make it meaty with a chopped cooked sausage, bits of bacon or leftover cooked chicken.

Makes 1 pizza

1 ready-made flour tortilla
oil for frying
2 spring onions, chopped
4 mushrooms, sliced and fried
3 or 4 chargrilled courgette strips (see page 81)
quarter of a green pepper, sliced
seasoning to taste
1 tbsp tomato passata (page 97)
1 tsp dried herbs
cheese, sliced or grated (any kind or a mixture)

Preheat the oven to 200°C (Gas Mark 6).

Heat a heavy-based frying pan and dry-fry the tortilla for about 1 minute on each side.

Place the tortilla on a shallow baking tray. Spread the passata over the tortilla then add the vegetables in an even layer. Sprinkle over the dried herbs and top with cheese. Bake in the oven for about 10 minutes until the cheese melts and starts to colour.

Slow-roast pork belly, apple sauce and black pudding bruschetta

This is the perfect way to use up any excess pork belly from the slow-roast recipe on page 108. I reckon the combination of tender pork belly, apple sauce and black pudding is one of the world's greatest food combos. Try it on anything from bite-sized crostini (page 54) to a full-length baguette for a satisfying open sarnie experience.

Makes 10 bruschetta

For the apple sauce:
200g cooking apples, peeled, quartered, cored and chopped
1 tbsp caster sugar
2 tbsp water
1 tsp lemon juice

leftover slow-roast pork belly (page 108), cut into slices
2 tbsp stock or water
a few slices black pudding
oil for frying

1 baguette, cut on a slight diagonal into 10 slices about 1½cm thick
olive oil
seasoning
leftover crackling

Preheat the oven to 180°C (Gas Mark 4).

First make the apple sauce. Place the apple pieces in a saucepan with the sugar and water and lemon juice and cook gently on a low heat for about 10 minutes, until the apples start to collapse but still retain texture.

Place the pork belly slices in an ovenproof dish and cover with foil. Heat in the oven until just warmed through, about 5 minutes.

Meanwhile, gently fry the black pudding slices in a little oil for about 2 minutes on each side. Sprinkle the baguette slices with olive oil, sea salt and freshly ground pepper, and lightly toast on both sides.

To serve, pile some pork belly on each of the toasted baguette slices, add a dollop of apple sauce and top with a slice of black pudding. Don't forget to offer a bowl of crackling, if you haven't already eaten it all.

Sausage, courgettes and peas in tomato sauce

This dish came about when I got home from a weekend away giving cooking demos. An artisan butcher had given me some fabulous rare-breed sausages and wicked dry cured bacon that I'd cooked at the show and now had left over. I also had leftover chargrilled courgettes and a load of peas from having to cook the whole bag because I didn't have a freezer. I found a few very squidgy tomatoes in my veg rack, half a roasted pepper in the fridge and a tin of tomatoes in the cupboard. Anyway, this is taste-driven comfort food. Don't get too hung up on the quantities or even the ingredients – adapt as you please.

Serves 4

oil for frying
2 onions, thinly sliced
1 tin chopped tomatoes
2 big handfuls of fresh tomatoes, roughly chopped
1 dsp tomato purée
1 tbsp dried herbs
1 mug chicken stock
half a roasted red pepper, roughly chopped
4 chargrilled courgette strips (page 81)
1 mug cooked peas
6 cooked sausages, sliced
6 cooked bacon rashers, roughly chopped

Heat a little oil in a large saucepan over a medium heat. Add the onions and gently cook for 15-20 minutes until caramelised.

Add the tomato purée and cook for a further 2 minutes. Then add the tinned and chopped tomatoes, and cook over a medium heat for 10-15 minutes.

Add the herbs, chicken stock, roasted pepper, courgette strips, peas, sausages and bacon. Simmer for 10 minutes then serve with crusty bread or pasta.

Chicken and pea biryani

This 'dry' rice dish (pictured on page 123) is one of the quickest, easiest and tastiest ways to use up a whole stack of random refrigerated cooked leftovers. The rice forms the base of the dish – the remaining ingredients are up to you.

Makes 1 big portion

oil for frying
half an onion, finely chopped
½ tsp turmeric
½ tsp ground cumin
pinch of chilli flakes
half a mug long-grain rice
1 mug water or stock
handful of cooked chicken (or meat of your choice)
half a mug cooked peas

Heat 1 tbsp oil in a saucepan and gently fry the onion for a few minutes until soft. Add the turmeric, cumin and chilli flakes and cook for a further minute, stirring constantly. Add the rice and stir for a minute before adding the water or stock. Reduce the heat and simmer with the lid on for about 7 minutes.

Add the chicken and the peas to the pan then remove from the heat and allow to stand with the lid on for a further 7 minutes. Serve immediately or eat cold as a salad.

Spag bol revisited

Don't lose it – use it! This is a classic example of the tail end of one meal becoming the inspiration for the next one, and the ultimate in leftovers recycling.

Four uses for two tablespoons of spag bol

★ *In hollowed-out tomatoes. Slice off the top of the tomatoes and carefully remove the juice and pulp. Combine it with the leftover spag bol, divide the mixture between the tomatoes and (ideally) grate over a little Parmesan. Place the tomato lids on top and bake in the oven for 10 minutes.*

★ *In an omelette – pasta and all! Simply heat the spag bol and pour into the omelette just before folding and serving. See page 42 for the perfect omelette.*

★ *In bread tart cases (page 56), topped with cheese and grilled until melting – pictured on page 139.*

★ *Spag bol pasty. See the leftover roast dinner recipe on page 142.*

Bubble and squeak

This is a classic leftover recipe for the most basic of cheap staples: potatoes and cabbage. However, you can create your own customised versions with all sorts of other leftovers such as bacon, sausage, green beans and sprouts. They make a fantastic breakfast treat topped with fried, poached or scrambled egg – especially with sausage and bacon.

Serves 4

350g leftover mashed potato
250g cabbage, cooked and shredded
seasoning to taste
1 tbsp oil for frying

Combine the mash, cabbage and seasoning in a bowl. Divide into 4 patties. Heat the oil in a frying pan and fry the patties for about 5 minutes on each side until golden brown. Serve immediately.

For other recipe ideas cooked leftovers, see:

Yorkshire puddings: five gourmet Yorkshire pudding fillings (page 35)
Pancakes: four tempting pancake fillings (page 36)
Mini bread tart cases (page 56)
Lettuce: five little gem lettuce boats (leftover biryani) (page 128)

The fruit bowl

When it comes to getting truly wasted, the fruit bowl gives the veg rack a proper run for its money. How many times have you filled that fruit bowl with plump, juicy, shiny specimens, confident in the determination to change your ways? Then a week or two later, with bowed head and slumped shoulders, you find yourself depositing the entire contents into the bin while the gods of fresh fruit try to choke you with a green plume of musty powder. Face it, with the best will in the world you're never going to get through that enormous pile of kiwi fruit, even if they were just a quid, or a second punnet of nectarines just because you only had to pay for one. So, given this oh-too-familiar scenario, how do you reverse such an ingrained pattern of behaviour?

Mixed fruit

The 'buy one get one free' deal that proliferates supermarket shelves is perhaps the biggest contributory factor to throwing away fruit. The problem is you simply can't eat that much fruit before it starts to ferment! Half the time it's under-ripe when you buy it, making it unusable for several days, and then suddenly you've got a glut. The secret is to start using it while still under-ripe. A simple stock syrup made up of sugar and water can turn rock-hard nectarines and peaches into soft, sweet fruit. In fact, this syrup will work on just about any fruit – even bananas – but I think peaches and nectarines benefit from it the most. For fabulous ways to use this delicious poached fruit, try pancakes (page 36) or instant croissant trifle (page 57).

Stock syrup The magic potion for transforming under-ripe fruits into juicy morsels in minutes! This poaching syrup can be flavoured with anything – cinnamon stick, star anise, orange peel, cloves – and can be used over and over again, generating even more flavour each time.

Place an equal volume of caster sugar and water into a pan, add your choice of flavourings, and heat until the sugar has dissolved. Add the fruit and poach at a very gentle simmer until tender. This will take around 5-15 minutes, depending on the ripeness of the fruit.

Fresh berry or soft fruit purée

Uses: soft fruit, icing sugar

This is when supermarket deals are a real advantage. Buy up those heavily reduced punnets of raspberries, strawberries and other soft fruit and make them into fantastic restaurant dessert sauces. Simply add icing sugar and blitz them with a stick blender with bowl attachment or a food processor. What a way to give a home-cooked makeover to a shop-bought dessert. Happy days!

Ultimate breakfast smoothie

After half a lifetime of tearfully throwing away mouldy fruit and skipping breakfast, I've finally come up with a winning formula for using it up and getting a tasty, nutritious breakfast to boot. I've done away with the fancy juicers and squeezers and the epic cleaning operation that accompanies them, and settled for the one jug blender. It pulses the chunkiest of fruit to smooth liquid in seconds and needs nothing more than a blast under the hot tap straight after use to fully clean.

The fruits listed here are just suggestions. I rarely use the same, and what I choose is generally dictated by supermarket reductions on fruit that is supposedly past its best. It's actually better than the pristine stuff, as it's got more flavour, colour and a better texture for a quick blast in the blender.

1 banana
2 kiwis
1 mango
3 tbsp low fat vanilla yogurt
1 tbsp instant oats
½ litre soya milk
1 dsp honey

Chop the fruit into your blender, add the other ingredients then whizz until smooth.

Bananas

There's probably more myth and mystery surrounding the banana than any other fruit. Very simply, certain fruits (including apples) emit ethylene gas, a ripening agent, and bananas produce lots. So if you want to soften hard avocados, pop them into a paper bag with a banana. If you don't want to over-ripen other fruit and veg, store them well away.

We've been conditioned by supermarkets to have a false impression of what a ripe banana actually is, which contributes to our binning them before their time is up. A ripe banana has a rich yellow-coloured skin streaked with black/brown markings – not pale yellow and without a blemish.

Chocolate-dipped banana lolly

Uses: banana, dark chocolate, wooden skewer

Here's an incredible thing. When you freeze a peeled banana, remove it from the freezer and leave it for a few minutes, it has the texture of ultra-smooth ice cream. If you didn't know better, you'd swear you were biting into scrummy banana-flavoured ice cream! Peel a banana and carefully insert a long wooden skewer lengthways so it sticks out of the bottom as a handle. Wrap the banana in foil or cling film and then freeze. Heat some dark chocolate in a bowl sat over a pan of simmering water. When the chocolate has melted, coat the frozen banana with it. Add streaks of melted white chocolate for top taste and presentation. Lay the banana on a piece of baking parchment in the fridge until the chocolate has set, then tuck in while the banana is still semi-frozen.

Apples

Apples The apple is one of those fruits that tend to be bought out of guilt. You know you should be eating them, but when it comes to the crunch, a banana is just so much easier on the mouth. The best way to get through that glut of apples is to turn them into a delicious dessert. Generally speaking, apples will last the longest stored in a clear plastic bag in the fridge. However, deteriorating apples will affect the others, so remove any rogue specimens as soon as possible.

Apple tarte tatin

Another example of a legendary recipe that's just as likely to be found in a traditional French kitchen as in an elegant Parisian patisserie. Such desserts may cause panic among those 'not in the know', but essentially it's just apples and ready-rolled puff pastry, with a bit of sugar and butter thrown in for good measure. And it's fine to use older apples, as the caramelisation process will disguise any slight wrinkles.

Makes 1 large tart (serves 6)

400g caster sugar
2 tbsp water
150g unsalted butter, cubed
3kg apples, peeled, halved, cored and cut into wedges
ready-rolled puff pastry, cut into a disc the size of the frying pan
icing sugar for dusting (optional)

You will also need: 30-36cm heavy-based, non-stick frying pan

Preheat the oven to 200°C (Gas Mark 6).

Place the sugar and water in a frying pan and gently melt over a low heat until it turns to a golden caramel. Remove from the heat and add the cubed butter, stirring in carefully.

Arrange the apples on top of the caramel, keeping them tightly packed together. Lay the sheet of pastry over the apples, tucking it in down the sides of the pan. Sprinkle the pastry with icing sugar and place in the preheated oven for 20 minutes, or until the pastry is golden brown. Remove from the oven and leave to rest for 1 minute.

Place a large plate or board over the pan and turn it out so the apples are face up. Be very careful when doing this as the caramel will be hot.

Apple, cinnamon and sultana filo

Filo pastry sounds scary, but in its ready-rolled supermarket form it couldn't be easier to use. It's another of those ingredients that can be stored in the freezer, ready to use as an edible wrap for sweet and savoury leftovers. Serve this scrummy dessert with a good dollop of crème fraîche, ice cream or whipped double cream.

Serves 4

600g apples, peeled and quartered, cores removed, each quarter cut into 6 chunks
150g butter
150g demerara sugar
150g sultanas
2 tsp ground cinnamon
200g filo pastry

Preheat the oven to 180°C (Gas Mark 4).

Melt 50g butter in a pan, then add all the other ingredients except the filo and the rest of the butter and cook gently for about 10 minutes, or until the apple is soft but still retains its shape. Remove from the heat and allow to stand for 30 minutes.

To prepare the filo, melt the remaining 100g butter in a pan. Take a 17 x 28cm sheet and lay on a work surface with the long edge running horizontally. Brush the whole sheet with melted butter, lay another sheet on top of the first and brush again with melted butter. Repeat one more time so you have 3 buttered layers.

Spread a quarter of the apple mixture evenly along the pastry, leaving a border of about 6cm at each end and 5cm top and bottom. Fold the ends of the pastry in towards the middle. Fold the bottom edge up and over and then roll, creating a spring roll-like cylinder.

Brush with more melted butter, and place on a baking tray lined with baking parchment. Cook the filo in the oven for about 25 minutes, or until the pastry is golden brown. Just beware of the hot filling if you can't wait to bite into it!

For other recipe ideas for fruit, see:

Change your thinking: salsatastic! (mango and courgette, and apple and celery) (page 16)
Instant croissant trifle (page 57)
Pancakes: four tasty pancake fillings (poached fruit and whipped cream) (page 36)

Index